HALLUCINATED CITY

MÁRIO DE ANDRADE

Hallucinated City

Translated and with an
introduction by Jack E. Tomlins

A bilingual facing edition

EMPYREAN SERIES No. 25

---

about   Andrade, Mário de. *Paulicéia Desvairada*.
             São Paulo: Casa Mayença, 1922.

             Hallucinated City. Translated by Jack E. Tomlins.
             Nashville: Vanderbilt UP, 1968

copyright   Translation © 2022 the heirs of Jack E. Tomlins

isbn   978-1-955190-65-7

CONTENTS

Introduction

vii

Hallucinated City

To Mário de Andrade

3

Extremely Interesting Preface

5

26	Inspiração • Inspiration	27
28	O Trovador • The Troubador	29
30	Os Cortejos • The Processions	31
32	A Escalada • The Escalade	33
36	Rua de São Bento • São Bento Street	37
40	O Rebanho • The Flock	41
44	Tiêtê • Tiêtê River	45
46	Paisagem N. 1 • Landscape 1	47
50	Ode ao Burguês • Ode to the Bourgeois Gentleman	51
56	Tristura • Sadness	57
60	Domingo • Sunday	61
64	O Domador • The Animal Tamer	65
68	Anhangabaú • Anhangabaú	69
72	A Caçada • The Hunt	73

78	Nocturno • Nocturne	79
84	Paisagem N. 2 • Landscape 2	85
88	Tu • You	89
92	Paisagem N. 3 • Landscape 3	93
94	Colloque Sentimental • Colloque Sentimental	95
98	Religião • Religion	99
102	Paisagem N. 4 • Landscape 4	103
106	As Enfibraturas do Ipiranga • The Moral Fibrature of the Ipiranga	107

Introduction

Jack E. Tomlins

> Enigmatic and profound Mário de Andrade!...
> who brought to us a true understanding of our
> lyricism, our true romantic soul, and our true
> poetic form—disinterestedly undisciplined—
> crying out a canticle of glory and liberation...
>
> WILSON MARTINS, *INTERPRETATIONS*

Since his untimely death in 1945 the Brazilian writer Mário Raul de Morais Andrade has become the object of ever-increasing interest to his own countrymen as well as to students of Brazilian culture in the English-speaking world. Literary historians and critics in both Americas study the role that he played in the early twenties as instigator and artificer of Brazil's most significant literary event of this century: the Modernist Movement. Of this Movement he has been variously named prophet, pope, and lawgiver. It has been repeatedly said of Mário de Andrade that it was he who most profoundly understood the spirit and the mission of Modernism and that it was he who, in his creative life, most effectively embodied the Modernism that he had helped to create. Still, the totality of the man—poet, novelist, critic, folklorist, musicologist—remains largely a mystery. Even the wisest historian of Brazilian Modernism admits that it is perhaps best to speak ultimately of Mário de Andrade as a presence, a man whose creative and critical personality genially hovered over the literary scene from 1922 to 1945.

The young poet was something more human than presence or myth, however, when he participated in the Week of Modern Art in his native São Paulo in February of 1922. Among the artists who took part in this series of three festivals devoted to modern Brazilian culture were sculptors, painters, writers, and musicians. Three separate sessions convened between February 13 and 17 in the Municipal Theatre. There *paulistas* stared bemused or aghast at the paintings of Anita Malfatti, the sculpture of Brecheret; they heard readings of modern Brazilian poetry and the music of Villa-Lobos. What today seems a quaint preview of things to come struck the Brazilian public of 1922 as wildly extravagant, insanely paranoiac.

In the years just before and after World War I, the young Brazilians, like the young North American writers, had gone to Europe. A tropical lost generation, they had come in contact with such liberated spirits as Jean Cocteau, Filippo Marinetti, Blaise Cendrars, Jean Epstein; they subsequently wanted a Brazilian art that was truly modern in the European aesthetic tradition they had recently discovered. They wanted at the same time an art that was authentically and thematically Brazilian. Such was the complex revolution of the Week of Modern Art and such the juncture at which Mário de Andrade purposefully entered the literary scene.

By 1922, Mário and his fellow poets had surveyed the literary landscape of their country, and they saw a horizon littered with volumes of played-out Symbolism and Parnassianism. Mário himself, in 1917, had paid his own debt to the old schools in his volume of youthful, imitative verse, *There is a Drop of Blood in Every Poem* (*Há uma Gota de Sangue em Cada Poema*). He continued to read the French poets—Verhaeren, Rimbaud. He learned from the former that the modern world, constantly animated by the press of violent human and social change, might admirably furnish the material of a new poetry. Both influenced and dazzled by Verhaeren, the Brazilian poet later conceived his own *paulista Villes Tentaculaires*: a volume of "modern" poems composed in free verse and devoted to his beloved São Paulo. During most of the year 1921 he was busy with the polishing of this volume, the *Hallucinated City* (*Paulicea Desvairada*). When he discovered that individual poems from the collection had an irritating effect on the overwhelmingly middle-class sensibilities of São Paulo, he knew it as time to bring his book before the general public and his fellow poets. This he did in the following July of 1922, the year of Modern Art.

Hallucinated City is a slender volume of twenty-two poems preceded by a short dedication from the poet to the poet and an "Extremely Interesting Preface", as Mário immodestly qualified his foreword. This preface, often called the bible of Brazilian Modernism, in reality constitutes the first formal poetics of the Movement. As such, it is largely responsible for the direction which the Brazilian lyric took after 1922. Rather than bible, the "Extremely Interesting Preface" might more justly be termed missal: text of the proper thing to write, rubric directing the creator as to how he shall write it.

The poet himself, however, would have objected to the term "missal". It smacks of school, and he hated the rigidity of the literary school. He remarked at the conclusion of his preface that in art, schools served the vanity of the founder-poet and merely emphasized the imbecility of the followers of the founder. Sheep after the shepherd. There is undoubtedly here the poet's constantly reiterated desire to divorce himself from the appellation of "Futurist", after the manner of Marinetti, a title which he had shortly before received from his fellow poet, Oswald de Andrade. With customary tongue-in-cheek, Mário states that in order to prove his divorcement from Futurism he will found his own school: Hallucinism. Next week he will found another.

This, in itself, is not to be taken seriously. What the Brazilian admired in Marinetti was the liberated word: "the suggestive, associative, symbolic, universal, and musical power of the liberated word". He did not, however, appreciate the petrification of the liberated word in a modern poetic system. This is the gulf that separates Mário from the Italian Futurist. This freedom from the stricture of school points always, in Mário, away from Futurism and toward Modernism. Unlike the Futurists, Mário writes of modern things only because they are part of his world; they are neither to be systematized nor to be deified. They are to be used as an extremely powerful auxiliary in the composition of modern poetry. So it is that in the *Hallucinated City* Brazil's first revolutionary Modernist writes of the Cadillac (belonging to Oswald), streetcars, factories, trains, airplanes: the complex ordure of modern civilization.

Although the poet shuns the rigidity of the school, he takes especial delight in his own literary theories:

a. Poetry is equated with lyricism. The two terms are synonymous. Lyricism is the same as the poet's inspiration: whatever his unconscious cries out to him, he writes down on paper. Art later enters the process to weed out all dull repetition, romantic sentimentality, or useless detail.

b. Colorful exaggeration is perfectly suited to the lyric. Neither Homer nor Shakespeare hesitated to employ the daring image, the extravagant figure of speech.

c. The true lyric poet should never be restrained by such useless bonds as metrics, rhyme, or grammar.

Free verse is the ideal; however, the modern poet will not eschew the standard and traditional meters if it happens that he can, at the moment of creation, cast the tumultuous passions of his life in those old-fashioned molds. After all, modern poetry can well be made with old-fashioned subjects. The modern poet is not bound to write solely of gasoline and asphalt.

d. The modern lyric should follow the historical development of music in the progression: melody, harmony, polyphony. Melodic verse is the old-fashioned, nineteenth-century declarative statement, containing a complete thought:

São Paulo is a stage for Russian ballets.

Harmonic verse is the combination of distinct words which bear no immediate relationship to one another and, therefore, do not form a logical series:

Pack of dogs . . . Stock Market . . . Gambling . . .

Polyphonic verse is the combination not of words, as above, but rather of distinct phrases to achieve the same effect as harmonic verse:

The gears palsy . . . The mist snows . . .

Thus is expressed Mário's version of literary simultaneism put to the service of the lyrical impulse.

e. Lyric poetry should never be read by "mute eyes". The modern lyric poet writes his verses down so that subsequently they may be "sung, bellowed, wept" as they were at the moment of creation.

f. Finally, Mário admits that he did none of this theorizing at the moment of inspiration. Probably his theories are "not worth a damn." He only recalls that he "wept, sang, laughed, and bellowed." He was most alive when he set his inner turmoil down on paper in the form of lyric poetry. That was quite enough for him. He condemns schools and theories for what they are worth.

In a lecture delivered twenty years after the publication of the *Hallucinated City*, the poet recalled the events that immediately led to the composition of the poems in that volume. In 1920 he and his fellow poets had recently discovered the sculptor Victor Brecheret, who at that time had returned from his studies in Italy just as Anita Malfatti had returned before the War from her expressionist and cubist experiences in Germany. At great expense to his pocketbook, Mário was able to purchase a "Bust of Christ" from the sculptor, who was then all the rage among the young artists of São Paulo. Mário recalls proudly unwrapping his acquisition in the bosom of the family:

> There was the devil to pay. They yelled and screamed. That monstrosity was a mortal sin, screeched my old auntie the matriarch of the family. Who ever heard of a Christ with braids!

Hideous! Frightful! Maria Luisa, your son is totally depraved.

I was delirious, I swear. I honestly wanted to whack someone. I ate alone in an unbelievable state of distress. Later, at dusk, I went up to my room with the intention of pulling myself together, going out, relaxing a bit, setting off a bomb at the middle of the world. I recall that I went to the balcony, looked down at the square below without actually seeing it. Noises, lights, the ingenuous bantering of the taxi drivers: they all floated up to me. I was apparently calm and was thinking about nothing in particular. I don't know what suddenly happened to me. I went to my desk, opened a notebook and wrote down a title that had never before crossed my mind: *Hallucinated City*. After almost a year of soul-searching anguish, the explosion had come at last. In the midst of disappointments, pressing labors, debts, arguments, in a little more than a week I had scrawled on paper a barbaric canticle maybe twice as long as it was to be after I had cleared out all extraneous material.

Thus it was that the first authentically revolutionary and significant volume of Modernist verse was born. Owing to the nature of its genesis, it is not surprising that, like all the representative lyrical works of the first decade of

Brazilian Modernism, the *Hallucinated City* is, to a certain extent, a flawed book. It represents perhaps too much the impassioned outcry of the moment, notwithstanding Mário's definition of Art. This verse frequently lacks philosophical depth; it often reveals a want of simple meditation. On the other hand, it is legitimately the portrait of a young poet with all the baggage of his sincerity weighing lightly on his back. Later, in 1931, Mário was to write that, in his opinion, youths under twenty-five should be prohibited by law from publishing books of poetry! His final word on that point.

Nonetheless, if the poems which figure in the *Hallucinated City* had been deeply meditated and meditative, the work would have lacked the agitated revolutionary spirit so essential to the renovation of Brazil's fading Parnassianism. It is not foolhardy, when, to declare that this small volume of poetry was effectively instrumental in changing the direction of Brazilian letters for all time. After the Hallucinated City and the Modernist revolution followed the more durable and mature Modernist spirit. Brazilian Portuguese became once and for all a fitting tool for the composition of the lyric and the novel. The sociological prose fiction of the Northeast, largely a product of the thirties, would not have been possible without the literary housecleaning of the poets of the twenties. Because Mário de Andrade sang a vehement hymn of love to his São Paulo—and by extension to his Brazil—the path was opened to all

Brazilian writers to compose such hymns, each in his way, with varying degrees of profundity. And so they did.

The poems in the *Hallucinated City* have weathered the years since 1922 with admirable vigor and freshness because they are essentially good and honest verses. From the outset, in the first poem of the collection, Mário states his "Inspiration":

> São Paulo! tumult of my life...
> Gallicism crying in the wilderness of America!

He had clarified this point in his Preface: São Paulo is his love and his agitation, and he sings of this passion with a Gallic voice untainted by Italian Futurism.

His vision of São Paulo is, of course, hallucinated as it is flashed through a surrealistic prism. It must be noted, however, that the simultaneous images of Mário's private surrealism are always orderly and structural within the framework, or formality, of the individual poem. Ledo Ivo speaks of the poet as a "glosser of lucid and workaday moments" and describes the *Hallucinated City* as a "collection of the most lucid, rational and well-planned poems in all of Modernism."

One scene rapidly follows another, like a nude descending a staircase, like delirious motion picture images. The overall blurred impression on the retina, however, proceeds from an ingenious series of daring images:

> ... the gray of the goose-fleshed streets
> chats a lament with the wind ...
>
> ... a sorcerer sun is shattered
> in a Persian triumph of emeralds, topazes,
>   and rubies ...
>
> Nude bronze statues eternally coursing,
> in a fixed disdain for velocities ...
>
> ... the trolleys pass by like a skyrocket,
> clicking their heels on the tracks ...
>
> The sky is all a conventional battle
>   of white confetti;
> and the gray wildcats of the mountains in
>   the distance ...
>
> The little pigeons [girls] from the Normal School
> flutter between the fingers of the mist ...
>
> And the grand golden chorus of sacks of coffee!

Out of this paradoxical combination of the bleary and the brilliant, Mário de Andrade fashioned his little book. In it he jeered the drudgery of middle-class existence, governmental hypocrisy, and the destructive self-satisfaction of the masses. He gloried in his racy Brazilian language and gave it dignity. He danced a lyrical harlequinade and, like the sprite in diamond tights, he rejoiced in his freedom. Toward the end of his life, when the clowning and prancing were over, he glanced back. In the midst of a vigorous literary career, he spoke of himself and his companions with the balance and consummate good sense that had always characterized his creative efforts:

> I think that we Modernists of the Week of Modern Art should serve as an example to no one. However, we may well serve as a lesson… Human life is something other than arts and sciences and professions. It is in that other life that freedom has some meaning. Freedom is not a prize; it is a sanction. Yet to come.

    J. E. T.
    Nashville, Tennessee
    Feast of the Transfiguration, 1967

Acknowledgments

The editors would like to extend our thanks to Dr. José I. Suárez for his help in bringing this volume to fruition, and to Linda Turpin for granting us permission to bring her late husband's superb translations to a new generation of readers. As Jack Tomlins dedicated the original translation to Linda, so do we dedicate this volume.

HALLUCINATED CITY

To Mário de Andrade

Beloved Master,

In the many brief hours which you made me spend at your side, you often spoke of your faith in free and sincere art; and I received the courage of my Truth and pride in my Ideal not from myself but from your experience. Allow me now to offer you this book which came to me from you. Please God, may you never be vexed by the brutal doubt of Adrien Sixte...

However, I do not know, Master, whether you will forgive me the distance that lies between these poems and your noblest lessons... Forgive the efforts of the only one you chose for your disciple; of him who, at this moment of martyrdom, though fearfully, still regards you as his Guide, his Master, his Lord.

> Mário de Andrade
> December 14, 1921
> São Paulo

Extremely Interesting Preface

In my land of bile and gold
I follow the law.

E. VERHAEREN

Reader:
 Hallucinism has been launched.
 This preface—although interesting—useless.
 A few facts. Not all of them. No conclusions. For those who accept me, both facts and conclusions are useless. The curious will have the pleasure of discovering my conclusions, by comparing the work with the facts. As for those who reject me, it is wasted effort to explain to them what they have rejected even before they have read it.
 When I feel the lyric impulse upon me, I write without thinking all that my unconscious shouts out to me. I think afterward: not only to correct but also to justify what I have written. Hence the reason for this Extremely Interesting Preface.
 Furthermore, in this kind of chit-chat it is very difficult to know where the *blague* leaves off and the serious begins. I do not even know myself.
 And forgive me for being so behind the times

regarding present-day artistic movements. I am old-fashioned, I confess. No one can liberate himself once and for all from the grandaddy-theories he has imbibed, and the author of this book would be a hypocrite if he pretended to represent a modern orientation which as yet he himself does not totally comprehend.

A book obviously impressionistic. Now, according to the moderns, a grave error, Impressionism. The architects flee from the Gothic style as well as from the new art, allying themselves — beyond historical time — with elemental shapes: cube, sphere, etc. The painters scorn Delacroix as well as Whistler and take refuge in the constructive serenity of Raphael, Ingres, el Greco. In sculpture Rodin is horrendous; imaginary Africans are good. The musicians despise Debussy: genuflections before the cathedral polyphony of Palestrina and Johann Sebastian Bach. Poetry... "tends to despoil man of all his contingent and ephemeral aspects in order to grasp the humanity in him." I am old-fashioned, I confess.

"This Koran is nothing more than a jumble of confused and incoherent dreams. It is not inspiration drawn from God, but created by the author. Muhammed is not a prophet; he is a man who writes verses. Let him represent himself as some revealing sign of his destiny, like the ancient prophets." Perhaps they will say of me what they said of the creator of Allah. A notable difference between the two of us: Muhammed represented himself as a prophet; I have deemed it more proper to represent myself as a madman.

Have you read St. John the Evangelist? Walt Whitman? Mallarmé? Verhaeren?

For almost ten years I metrified and rhymed. Example?

ARTIST

I fain would paint-like Leonardo be,
Whose art in pious scenes refined became;
The vast corolla unto worldly fame
I'd ope of this exalted dream in me…

I yearn upon life's backdrop dun to see
Venetian tints the murkiness inflame
To give in rose and gold, as alms, the same
Fair tones where'er the stone and thistle be.

When I shall find that tinted fountainhead
And brush sublime, oh Veronese, borne
By you upon the upraised frieze o'erhead,

I'll in the land where Sorrows dwell sojourn;
And I shall live by painting smiles of red
Upon the lips of those who curse or mourn.

Senhores Laurindo de Brito, Martins Fontes, and Paulo Setúbal published their verses, although they obviously do not have the scope of Vicente de Carvalho or Francisca Julia. And they do very well. I could, like them, publish my metrical poetry.

I am not a Futurist (after Marinetti). I have said so before and I repeat it. I have points of contact with Futurism. When Oswald de Andrade called me a Futurist, he was wrong. The fault was mine. I knew of the existence of his article, and I allowed it to be published. The scandal was so great that I wished the whole world dead.

I was vain. I was trying to break free of obscurity. Today I am proud. I would not mind returning to obscurity. I thought my aims would be discussed. Even now I do not remain silent. They would mock my silence as much as they mock this uproar. I shall go through life with my arms outstretched, like the *L'indifférent* of Watteau.

"When some readers read these phrases (the poetry quoted), they did not understand immediately. I even think that it is impossible, without a bit of practice, to understand entirely, on a first reading, thoughts schematized in this way. But it is not for that reason that a poet can complain about his readers. Where these readers are contemptible is in their not thinking that a writer who signs his work does not write asininities for the sheer joy of testing his ink; and that beneath that apparent extravagance there was perhaps some extremely interesting significance, that there was something to understand." Jean Epstein.

There is in this world a gentleman named Zdislas Milner. And he wrote the following: "The fact that a work departs from already learned precepts and rules does not give the measure of its value." Excuse me for granting some value to my book. No father will abandon his hunchback child, who is drowning, to save the beautiful heir of his neighbor, for the simple reason that he is a father. The wet nurse who did so in the story was a completely unnatural ham.

Every writer believes in the worth of what he writes. If he shows it, it is out of vanity. If he does not show it, it is also out of vanity.

I do not flee from the ridiculous. I have illustrious companions.

The ridiculous is often subjective. It does not depend on the greater or lesser goal of the one who suffers it. We create it in order to garb in it the person who wounds our pride, ignorance, or sterility.

A little theory?

I believe that lyricism, born in the subconscious, purified into a clear or confused thought, creates phrases which are entire verses, without the necessity of counting so many syllables with predetermined accentuation. Run-on lines are a welcome respite to those poets who are trapped in the alexandrine prison. There are only rare examples of that in this book. As the twig is bent...

Inspiration is short-lived, violent. Any obstacle whatever upsets it and even silences it. When Art is added to Lyricism to create Poetry, this process does not consist of halting the mad dash of the lyric state in order to warn it of the stones and barbed-wire fences along the road. Let it stumble, fall, and wound itself. Art is a subsequent weeding out of all irksome repetitions, romantic sentimentalities, and useless or unexpressive details.

Let Art, therefore, not consist of ridding verses of colorful exaggerations. Exaggeration: ever-new symbol of life as well as of the dream. Through exaggeration, life and dreams are linked. And, employed consciously, it is not a defect, rather a legitimate means of expression.

"The wind sits in the shoulder of your sail!" Shakespeare. Homer had long ago written that the earth groaned beneath the feet of men and horses. But you must know that there are millions of exaggerations in the works of the masters.

Taine said that the artist's ideal consists of "presenting not the objects themselves, but rather of presenting clearly and completely any essential and outstanding characteristic of them, by means of the systematic alteration of the natural relationship between their parts, so as to make that characteristic more visible and dominant." However, I recognize that Senhor Luis Carlos has the right to quote the same thing in defense of his "Columns".

Have you ever thought about so-called "hideous

beauty"? That is too bad. Hideous beauty is a subterfuge created according to the size of the ears of certain philosophers to justify the attraction which the hideous exercises, at all times, over the artist. Do not come to me and say that the artist, reproducing the ugly, the hideous, is creating a beautiful work. To call beautiful that which is ugly and hideous, only because it is expressed with intensity, agitation, or art, is either to devalue or to ignore the concept of beauty. But "ugly" equals "sin." It is attractive. Anita Malfatti was talking to me the other day about the ever-new charm of the ugly. Anita Malfatti has undoubtedly not yet read Emile Bayard: "The logical purpose of a canvas is to be pleasing to the eye. However, artists take delight in expressing the singular charm of ugliness. The artist makes everything sublime."

Beauty in art: arbitrary, conventional, transitory: a matter of fashion. Beauty in nature: immutable, objective, natural. It possesses whatever eternity nature may possess. Art does not succeed in imitating nature, nor is this its object. All the great artists, whether consciously (the Raphael of the Madonnas, the Rodin of the Balzac, the Beethoven of the *Pastoral*, the Machado de Assis of the *Braz Cubas*) or unconsciously (the greater part of them) were deformers of nature. From which I infer that artistic beauty will be more artistic, more subjective, the more it withdraws from natural beauty. Let others infer what they will. I could not care less.

Our senses are fragile. Our perception of external things is dim, obstructed by a thousand veils which derive from our physical and moral defects: illness, prejudice, indisposition, antipathy, ignorance, heredity, circumstances of time and place, etc... Only ideally can we conceive of objects as acts in their beautiful or in their ugly integrity. Even when art derives its themes from the objective world, it is developed through comparisons which are remote, exaggerated, without apparent exactitude; or it indicates objects, as universals, without any qualifying delimitation whatever. It has the power of leading us to that free, musical idealization. This free and subjective idealization permits one to create a whole atmosphere of ideal realities where sentiments, beings and things, beauties and defects, are presented in their heroic plenitude, which surpasses the defective perception of the senses. I do not know what kind of Futurism can exist in one who practically embraces the aesthetic concepts of Fichte. Let us flee from nature! Only in this way will art not be offended by the ridiculous weakness of photography... colored.

I am no longer amused at all by the fact that people submit their emotions to the couch of Procrustes in order to obtain a conventional number of syllables in conventional rhythm. In my first book, I indifferently used several meters, without feeling any obligation to employ only regular meter. Now I free myself also from that preconception. I acquire others. Should I be scorned because of that?

I do not shun the dancer's trained balance found in *redondilhas* and decasyllables. It happens sometimes that emotions fit into those molds. Sometimes they go, then, into the rhythmic cabaret of my verses! In this question of meter, I am not an ally; I am like Argentina: I grow rich.

Concerning order? As a matter of fact, I am disgusted by what Musset called: "L'art de servir à point un dénouement bien cuit."[1]

There is the order of children leaving school, two by two, holding hands. There is the order of students in the upper grades going downstairs, four at a time, prettily jostling one another. There is the even higher order of the unleashed fury of the elements.

He who lectures on Brazilian history will follow an order which surely does not consist in studying the Paraguayan War before the illustrious discovery of Pedro Alvares. He who sings his subconscious will follow the unforeseen order of his emotions, of the association of images, of external contacts. It happens that the theme sometimes gets off the track.

The lyric impulse cries out inside us like the madding crowd. It would be highly amusing if we said to the crowd: "Slow down there! Let each cry out when it is his turn; and let the one who has the strongest argument keep it for the end!" The crowd is apparent confusion. He who knows

---

1. "The art of serving rare a well-done denouement." —Ed.

how to withdraw ideally from the confusion will see the imposing development of that collective soul speaking the exact rhetoric of vindication.

My vindication? Freedom. I use it; I do not abuse it. I know how to bridle it for my philosophical and religious truths, because philosophical and religious truths are not conventional like art: they are true. I do not abuse to that degree. I do not pretend to make anyone follow me. I am accustomed to going it alone.

Virgil and Homer did not use rhyme. Virgil and Homer have admirable assonances.

The Brazilian language is one of the richest and most sonorous. And it possesses that really splendid sound *ão*.

Marinetti was wonderful when he rediscovered the suggestive, associative, symbolic, universal, and musical power of the liberated word. Beyond that: it is as old as Adam. Marinetti was wrong: he made a system out of the liberated word. It is merely an extremely powerful auxiliary. I employ liberated words. I feel that my cup is too large for me, and yet I drink from the cups of others.

I am capable of constructing ingenious theories. Do you want to see one? Poetics is far more backward than music. Maybe even before the eighth century, music abandoned the regimen of melody, which at most dared to use octaves, in order to enrich itself with the infinite resources of harmony. Poetics, with rare exception down to the middle of the nineteenth century in France, was essentially melodic. I consider melodic verse the same as musical melody: a horizontal arabasque of consecutive tones (sounds) which contain intelligible thought. Now, if instead of using only verses which are horizontally melodic, such as:

> Mnesarete, the divine, the pale Phryne
> Appears before the austere and stern assembly
> of the supreme Areopagus...

we have words follow each other without any immediate connection among themselves, these words, for the very reason that they do not follow intellectually and grammatically, overlie one another for the gratification of our senses, and no longer form melodies but rather harmonies. I shall explain more fully. Harmony: combination of sounds. Example:

> "Ravishments... Struggles... Arrows...
> Songs... Populate!"

These words have no connection. They do not form a series. Each one is a phrase, an elliptical period, reduced to the telegraphic minimum. If I pronounce "Ravishments," since it does not belong to a phrase (melody), the word calls our attention to its detachment and it continues to vibrate, waiting for a phrase which will give it meaning, a phrase which does not follow. "Struggles" gives no conclusion whatever to "Ravishments"; and, under the same conditions, as we are not made to forget the first word, it continues to vibrate along with the other word. The other voices do the same. Thus: instead of melody (grammatical phrase) we have an arpeggiated chord, harmony—the harmonic verse. But, if instead of using only disconnected words, I use disconnected phrases, I get the same sensation of overlay, not now of words (notes) alone but of phrases (melodies). Hence: poetic polyphony. Thus in *Hallucinated City*, are employed melodic verse:

"São Paulo is a stage for Russian ballets";

harmonic verse:

"Pack of dogs ... Stock Market ... Gambling ...";

poetic polyphony (one and sometimes two and even more consecutive verses):

"The gears palsy ... The mist snows ...";

And so? Do not forget, however, that another will come along to destroy everything that I have constructed here.
Add this to theory:

1

The poetic geniuses of the past succeeded in giving greater importance to melodic verse by making it more beautiful, more varied, more moving, more surprising. Some even succeeded in formulating harmonies, at times extremely rich. Harmonies, nonetheless, unconscious, sporadic. I can prove the unconscious part: Victor Hugo, very often harmonic, exclaimed after he had heard the Quartet from *Rigoletto*: "Just let them make it possible for me to combine several phrases simultaneously and they'll see what I'm capable of." I find the anecdote in Galli, *Aesthetics of Music.* Se non é vero...

2

There are certain figures of speech in which we can see the embryo of oral harmony, just as we find the germ of musical harmony in the reading of the symphonies of Pythagoras. Antithesis: genuine dissonance. And if it is so greatly appreciated, that is proper because poets, like musicians, have always felt the great charm of dissonance, of which G. Migot speaks.

3

Commentary on the words of Hugo. Oral harmony is not effected, like musical harmony, in the senses, because words are not fused like notes; rather they are shuffled together, and they become incomprehensible. The creation of poetic harmony is effected in the intellect. The comprehension of the arts expressive of the succession of time is never immediate, rather it is intermediate. In the diachronic arts we coordinate consecutive acts of the memory which we assimilate in a final whole. This whole, the result of successive states of mind, renders the final and complete comprehension of music, poetry, and finished dance. Victor Hugo was wrong when he wished to effect objectively that which is effected subjectively within ourselves.

4

Psychologists will not accept the theory. Merely answer them with the "Só-quem-ama" by Bilac. Or with Heine's verses from which Bilac derived the "Só-quem-ama". If, perhaps, some shocking and unforeseen thing has happened to you (it has, naturally), recall the disordered tumult of the many ideas which at that moment coursed through your brain. Those ideas, reduced to the telegraphic minimum of the word, did not persevere because they did not belong to any sentence; they had no reply, solution, or continuity. They quivered, echoed, massed, heaped. Without juncture, with no apparent agreement—although they were born of the same occurrence—they formed, in rapid succession, true simultaneity, true harmonies accompanying the energetic and grand melody of the occurrence.

5

The Bilac of *Tarde* often represents an attempt at poetic harmony. Hence, in part at least, the new style of the book. He discovered for the Brazilian language that particular poetic harmony rarely employed before him. (Gonçalves Días brilliantly in the fight scene, Y-Juca-Pirama). Bilac's defect lay in the fact that he did not methodize his finding, did not extract all the consequences of it. His defect can be explained historically: *Tarde* is an apogee. Decadence does not follow apogee. Apogee is already decadence, because, since it is stagnation, it cannot in itself contain progress, an ascending evolution. Bilac represents a destructive phase in poetry, because all perfection in art signifies destruction. I can imagine your alarm, reader, as you read this. I do not have time to explain: study it, if you will. Our primitivism represents a new constructive phase. It falls to us to schematize and methodize the lessons of the past. I will return to the poet. He behaved like the creators of the medieval Organum: he accepted the harmonies of fourths and fifths while scorning thirds, sixths, and all the other intervals. The number of his harmonies is extremely restricted. Thus "... the air and the earth, the flora and fauna, the grass and the bird, the stone and the trunk, the nests and the ivy, the water and the reptile, the leaf and the insect, the flower and the beast" gives the impression of a long and monotonous series of medieval fifths: boring, excessive, useless, incapable of stimulating the hearer and giving him the feeling of dusk in the forest.[2]

Lyricism: a sublime affective state — the next thing to sublime madness. Preoccupation with metrics and rhyme hinders the free naturalness of objectified lyricism. Therefore sincere poets confess that they have never written their best verses. Rostand, for instance; and, among us, more or less, Senhor Amadeu Amaral. I have the good fortune of writing my best verses. Better than that I cannot do.

Ribot said somewhere that inspiration is a telegram in code sent by unconscious activity to conscious activity which decodes it. Both the poet and the reader may share that conscious activity. In this way the poet does not denude or thoroughly analyze the lyric moment, and he magnanimously concedes to the reader the glory

---

[2]. Some six or eight months ago, I explained this theory to my friends. Now, in December, I receive the November issues, numbers 11 and 12, of the journal *Esprit Nouveau*. Speaking of *Esprit Nouveau*: my crutches in this Extremely Interesting Preface. Epstein, continuing his study "The Literary Phenomenon", observes modern harmonism which he denominates "simultaneism". He finds that it is interesting, but he says that it is "physiological Utopia". Epstein falls into the same error that Hugo fell into.

of collaborating in the poems.

"Language permits the ambiguous form which marble does not permit." Renan.

"Between the plastic artist and the musician stands the poet who approaches the plastic artist with his conscious production, while he achieves the possibilities of the musician in the dark depths of the unconscious." Wagner.

You are beginning to see how accustomed I am to going it alone...

Sir Lyricism, when he disembarked from the El Dorado of the Unconscious at the pier of the Land of the Conscious, is inspected by the ship's doctor, Intelligence, who cleanses him of quirks and of all sickness whatsoever that might spread confusion and obscurity in this progressive little land. Sir Lyricism undergoes one more visit from the customs officials, a visit discovered by Freud who called it Censorship. I am a smuggler! I am against the vaccination laws.

It appears that I am all instinct. That is not true. There is in my book—and it does not displease me—a pronounced intellectualist tendency. What do you expect? I smuggle my silk in without paying the duties. But it is psychologically impossible for me to liberate myself from vaccinations and tonics.

Grammar appeared after languages were organized. It so happens that my unconscious knows nothing of the existence of grammars or of organized languages. And my unconscious, like Sir Lyricism, is a smuggler....

You will easily note that if grammar is sometimes scorned in my poetry, it does not suffer serious insults in this Extremely Interesting Preface. Preface: skyrocket of my higher self. The poems: landscape of my deeper self.

Pronouns? I write Brazilian. If I use Portuguese orthography, it is because it furnishes me an orthography without altering the result.

In my opinion, to write modern art never means to represent modern life through its externals: automobiles, movies, asphalt. If these words frequent my book, it is not because I think that I write "modern" with them; but since my book is modern, these things have their reason for being in it.

Besides, I know that there may be a modern artist who seeks inspiration in the Greece of Orpheus or in the Lusitania of Nun'Alvares. I recognize furthermore the existence of eternal themes, open to adoption because of their modernity: universe, homeland, love and the presence-of-the-absent, ex-bitter-pleasure-of-wretches.

Neither did I seek to attempt insincere and cross-eyed primitivism. We are actually the primitives of a new epoch. Aesthetically: I sought an expression more human and more free from art among the hypotheses of psychologists, naturalists, and critics of the primitives of past ages.

The past is a lesson to be meditated, not to be imitated.

"E tu che sé costí, anima viva,
  Pártiti da cotesti che son morti."

For many years I sought myself. I have found myself. Do not tell me now that I seek originality because I have already discovered where it was: it belongs to me, it is mine.

When one of the poems in this book was published, many people told me: "I did not understand it." There were some, however, who confessed: "I understood it, but I did not feel it." As for my dear friends... I saw more than once that they felt it, but they did not understand it. Evidently my book is good.

A famous writer said about me and my friends that we were either geniuses or jackasses. I think that he is right. We feel, I as well as my friends, the desire to be showoffs. If we were sheep to the point of forming a collective school, this would surely be "Showoffism". Our desire: to illuminate. The extreme left in which we have stationed ourselves will not permit halfway solutions. If we are geniuses: we will point the road to follow; if we are jackasses: shipwrecks to avoid.

I sing in my own way. What do I care if no one understands me? You say that I do not have enough strength to universalize myself? What do I care! Singing to the accompaniment of the complex lute that I have constructed, I strike out through the wild jungle of the city. Like primitive man, at first I shall sing alone. But song is an engaging fellow: it gives rebirth in the soul of another man — predisposed or merely sincerely curious and free — to the same lyric state provoked in us by joys, sufferings, ideals. I shall always find some man or some woman who will be rocked in the hammock of the libertarian cadence of my verses. At that moment: a new, dark and bespectacled Amphion, I shall make the very stones rise up like a wall at the magic of my song. And within those walls we shall sequester our tribe.

My hand has written about this book that: "I neither had nor do I now have the slightest intention of publishing it." *Jornal do Comércio*, June 6. Read the words of Gourmont concerning contradiction: first volume of the *Promenades Littéraires*. Rui Barbosa has a lovely page on contradiction, I do not remember where. There are a few words also in Jean Cocteau, *La Noce Massacrée*.

But this whole preface, with all the nonsensical theories which it contains, is not worth a damn. When I wrote *Hallucinated City* I did not think about any of this. I guarantee, however, that I wept, sang, laughed, and bellowed... I am alive!

Besides, verses are not written to be read by mute eyes. Verses are meant to be sung, bellowed, wept. If you cannot sing, do not read "Landscape 1". If you cannot bellow, do not read "Ode to the Bourgeois Gentleman". If you cannot pray, do not read "Religion". Scorn: "The Escalade". Suffer: "Colloque Sentimental". Forgive: the lullaby, one of the solos of My Madness from "The Moral Fibrature". I will not go on. It disgusts me to hand over the key to my book. If you are like me, you already have the key.

So the poetic school of "Hallucinism" is finished.

In the next book I will found another school.

And I do not want disciples. In art: School equals the imbecility of the many for the vanity of a single man.

I could have quoted Gorch Fock. I would have been spared this Extremely Interesting Preface. "Every song of freedom is born in prison."

Inspiração

Onde até na força do verão havia
tempestades de ventos e frios de
crudelíssimos inverno.

FR. LUIS DE. SOUSA

São Paulo! comoção de minha vida...
Os meus amores são flores feitas de original!...
Arlequinal!... Trajes de losangos... Cinza e ouro...
Luz e bruma... Forno e inverno morno...
Elegâncias sutis sem escândalos. sem ciúmes...
Perfumes de Paris... Arys!
Bofetadas líricas no Trianon... Algodoal!...

São Paulo! comoção de minha vida...
Galicismo a berrar nos desertos da América.

Inspiration

Where even at the height of summer
there were storms of wind and cold
like unto the harshest winter.

FRA LUIS DE SOUSA

São Paulo! tumult of my life...
My loves are flowers made from the original...
Harlequinate!... Diamond tights... Gray and gold...
Light and mist... Oven and warm winter...
Subtle refinements without scandals, without jealousy...
Perfumes from Paris... Arys!
Lyrical slaps in the Trianon... Cotton field!...

São Paulo! tumult of my life...
Gallicism crying in the wilderness of America.

O Trovador

Sentimentos em mim do asperamente
dos homens das primeiras eras...
As primaveras de sarcasmo
intermitentemente no meu coração arlequinal...
Intermitentemente...
Outras vezes é um doente, um frio
na minha alma doente como um longo som redondo...
Cantabona! Cantabona!
Dlorom...

Sou um tupi tangendo um alaúde!

The Troubador

Sentiments in me of the harshness
of the men of the primeval epochs ...
The vernal seasons of sarcasm
intermittently in my harlequinate heart ...
Intermittently ...
Other times it is a sick man, a chill
in my sick soul like a long round sound ...
Cantabona! Cantabona!
Dlorom ...

I am a Tupi Indian strumming a lute!

Os Cortejos

Monotonias das minhas retinas...
Serpentinas de entes frementes a se desenrolar...
Todos os sempres das minhas visões! "Bon giorno, caro".

Horríveis as cidades!
Vaidades e mais vaidades...
Nada de asas! Nada de poesia! Nada de alegria!
Oh! os tumultuários das ausências!
Paulicéia—a grande boca de mil dentes;
e os jorros dentre a língua trissulca
de pus e de mais pus de distinção...
Giram homens fracos, baixos, magros...
Aerpentinas de entes frementes a se desenrolar...

Estes homens de São Paulo,
todos iguais e desiguais,
quando vivem dentro dos meus olhos tão ricos,
parecem-me uns macacos, uns macacos.

The Processions

Monotonies of my retinas...
Serpentines of quivering beings unrolling...
All the forevers of my visions! "Bon giorno, caro."

Horrid cities!
Vanities and more vanities...
No wings whatsoever! No poetry whatsoever!
    No joy whatsoever!
Oh! the agitatings of absences!
São Paulo—the great mouth with a thousand teeth;
and amidst the trifid tongue the torrents
of pus and more pus of distinction...
Men whirl past, feeble, short, skinny...
Serpentines of quivering beings unrolling...

These men of São Paulo,
all equal and unequal,
when they live within my eyes so rich,
seem to me just so many monkeys, just so many monkeys.

A Escalada

(Maçonariamente.)
—Alcantilações!... Ladeiras sem conto!...
Estas cruzes, estas crucificações da honra!...
—Não há ponto final no morro das ambições.
As bebedeiras do vinho dos aplaudires...
Champanhações... Cospe os fardos!

(São Paulo é trono.)—E as imensidões das escadarias!...
—Queres te assentar no píncaro mais alto? Catedral?...
—Estas cadeias da virtude!...
—Tripinga-te! (Os empurrões dos braços em segredo.)
Principiarás escravo, irás a Chico-Rei!

(Há fita de série no Colombo,
O Empurrão na Escuridão. Film nacional.)
—Adeus lírios do Cubatão para os que andam sozinhos!
(Sono tré tustune per i ragazzini.)
—Estes mil quilos da crença!...
—Tripinga-te. Alcançarás o sólio e o sol sonante!
Cospe os fardos! Cospe os fardos!
Vê que facilidades as tais asas?

The Escalade

(Freemasonrywise.)
—Escarpments!... Numberless hillsides!...
These crosses, these crucifixions of honor!...
—There is no terminal on the hill of ambitions.
The drunken sprees on the wine of applause...
Champagnations... Spit out your burdens!

(São Paulo is a throne.)—And the immensities
    of the staircases!...
—Do you want to sit on the highest pinnacle? Cathedral?
—These shackles of virtue!...
—Write the secret sign! (The elbow nudges in secret.)
You'll begin as a slave and become a Chico-Rei!

(There's a serial at the Colombo Theatre.
A Nudge in the Dark. Made in Brazil.)
—Farewell lilies of the Cubatão for those who walk alone!
(Sono tre tustune per i ragazzini.)
—These thousand kilos of belief!...
—Write the secret sign! You'll ascend the throne and
    the vibrant sun!
Spit out your burdens! Spit out your burdens!
Do you see how handy such wings are?...

(Toca a banda do Fieramosca: Pa, pa, pa, pum!
Toca a banda da polícia: ta, ra, ta, tchim!)
És rei! Olha O rei nu!
Que é dos teus fardos, Hermes Pança?!

—Deixei-os lá nas margens das escadarias,
Onde nas violetas corria o rio dos olhos de minha mãe...
—Sossega. És rico, és grandíssimo, és monarca!
Alguém agora t'os virá trazer.

(E ei-lo na curul do vêsgo Olho-na-Treva.)

(The Fieramosca band is playing: Pa, pa, pa, poom!
The police band is playing: Ta, ra, ta, cheem!)
You're a king! Behold the naked king!
Whatever happened to your burdens, Hermes Paunch?!

—I left them there beside the staircases,
Where the river of my mother's eyes ran in the violets ...
—Be calm. You're rich, you're magnificent,
    you're a monarch!
Someone will bring them back to you now.

(So behold him on the throne of the All-seeing
    Crossed Eye.)

Rua de São Bento

Triángulo.

Há navios de vela para os meus naufrágios!
E os cantares da uiara rua de São Bento...

Entre estas duas ondas plúmbeas de casas plúmbeas,
as minhas delicias das asfixias da alma!
Ha leilão. Ha feira de carnes brancas. Pobres arrozais!
Pobres brisas sem pelúcias lisas a alisar!
A cainçalha... A Bolsa... As jogatinas...

Não tenho navios de vela para mais naufrágios!
Faltam-me as fôrças! Falta-me o ar!
Mas qual! Não ha sequer um porto morto!
"Can you dance the tarantella?" — "Ach! ya."
São as califórnias duma vida milionária
numa cidade arlequinal...

O Clube Comercial... A Padaria Espiritual...
Mas a desilusão dos sombrais amorosos
põe *majoration temporaire*, 100%[nt]!...

São Bento Street

Triangle.

There are sailing vessels for my shipwrecks!
And the songs of the water-nymph street of São Bento...

Between these two leaden waves of leaden houses,
my delights in the asphyxias of the soul!
There is an auction. There is a white flesh market. Poor
    rice paddies!
Poor breezes without smooth plushes to smooth down!
Pack of dogs... Stock Market... Gambling...

I have no sailing vessels for more shipwrecks!
I've run out of strength! I've run out of breath!
What the hell! There isn't even a dead port!
"Can you dance the tarantella?" "Ach! ja."
They are the californias of a millionaire life
in a harlequinate city...

The Commercial Club... The Spiritual Bakery...
But the disillusion of the amorous shady places
puts *majoration temporaire*, 100 percent!

Minha Loucura, acalma-te!
Veste o *water-proof* dos tambéns!

Nem chegarás tão cedo
à fábrica de tecidos dos teus êxtases;
telefone: Além, 3991...
Entre estas duas ondas plúmbeas de casas plúmbeas,
vê, lá nos muito-ao-longes do horizonte,
a sua chaminé de céu azul!

My Madness, be calm!
Put on your raincoat of alsos!

Not for a long time will you arrive
at the textile factory of your ecstasies;
telephone number: Beyond 3991 ...
Between these two leaden waves of leaden houses,
behold, out there on the far-far-aways of the horizon,
its smokestack of blue sky!

O Rebanho

Oh! minhas alucinações!
Vi os deputados, chapéus altos.
sob o pálio vesperal, feito de mangas-rosas,
sairem de mãos dadas do Congresso...
Como um possesso num acesso em meus aplausos
aos salvadores do meu estado amado!...

Desciam inteligentes, de mãos dadas,
entre o trepidar dos taxis vascolejantes,
arua Marechal Deodoro...
Oh! minhas alucinações!
Como um possesso num acesso em meus aplausos
aos heróis do meu estado amado!...

E as esperanças de ver tudo salvo!
Duas mil reformas, tres projetos...
Emigram os futuros noturnos...
E verde, verde, verde!...
Oh! minhas alucinações!
Mas os deputados, chapéus altos,
Mudavam-se pouco a pouco em cabras!
Crescem-lhes os cornos, descem-lhes barbinhas...
E vi os chapéus altos do meu estado amado,

The Flock

Oh! my hallucinations!
I saw the deputies, high-hats,
beneath the vesperal canopy, made of pink mangoes,
issue from the Congress chambers holding hands...
Like one possessed in a fit by my applause
for the saviors of my beloved state!...

Intelligent, holding hands,
amidst the tremor of the shaking taxis,
they went down Marshal Deodoro Street...
Oh! my hallucinations!
Like one possessed in a fit by my applause
for the heroes of my beloved state!...

And the hopes of seeing everything safe!
Two thousand reforms, three projects...
Nocturnes as yet unborn flee from the city...
And green, green, green!...
Oh! my hallucinations!
But the deputies, high-hats,
Little by little changed into goats!
Their horns grow, their chin whiskers sprout...
And I saw that the high-hats of my beloved state,

com os triângulos de madeira no pescoço,
nos verdes esperanças, sob as franjas de ouro da tarde,
se punham a pastar
rente do palácio do senhor presidente...
Oh! minhas alucinações!

with the wooden triangles at their necks,
in the green hopes, beneath the golden tassels
    of the afternoon,
were beginning to graze
next to the palace of his honor the governor ...
Oh! my hallucinations!

Tiêtê

Era uma vez um rio...
Porém os Borbas-Gatos dos ultra-nacionais esperiamente!

Havia nas manhãs cheias de Sol do entusiasmo
as monções da ambição...
E as gigânteas vitórias!
As embarcações singravam rumo do abismal
    Descaminho...
Arroubos... Lutas... Setas... Cantigas... Povoar!...
Ritmos de Brecheret!... E a santificação da morte!
Foram-se os ouros!... E o hoje das turmalinas!...

—Nadador! Vamos partir pela via dum Mato-Grosso?
—Io! Mai!... (Mais dez braçadas.
Quina Migone. Hat Stores. Meia de seda.)
Vado a pranzare con la Ruth.

Tiêtê River

Once upon a time there was a river ...
But the Borbas-Gatos of the ultra-nationals
    country-clubbily!

There were on the mornings with the Sun of Enthusiasm
the monsoons of ambition ...
And the gigantic victories!
The boats sailed on to the unfathomable Corruption ...
Ravishments ... Struggles ... Arrows ... Songs ...
    Populate! ...
Rhythms of Brecheret! ... And the sanctification of death!
The gold has departed! ... And the today of the
    tourmalines! ...

"Swimmer! shall we set off toward a Mato-Grosso?"
"Io! Mai! ... (Ten more strokes.
 Quina Migone. Hat Stores. Silk stocking.)
 Vado a pranzare con la Ruth."

Paisagem N.º 1

Minha Londres das neblinas finas...
Pleno verão. Os dez mil milhões de rosas paulistanas.
Há neve de perfumes no ar.
Faz frio, muito frio...
E a ironia das pernas das costureirinhas
Parecidas com bailarinas...
O vento é como uma navalha
nas mãos dum espanhol. Arlequinal!...
Há duas horas queimou Sol.
Daqui a duas horas queima Sol.

Passa um São Bobo, cantando, sob os plátanos,
Um tralálá... A guarda-cívica! Prisão!
Necessidade a prisão
para que haja civilização?
Meu coração sente-se muito triste...
Enquanto o cinzento das ruas arrepiadas
dialoga um lamento com o vento...

Meu coração sente-se muito alegre!
Este friozinho arrebitado
dá uma vontade de sorrir!

Landscape 1

My London of the fine mists!
High summer. The ten thousand million roses of
    São Paulo.
There is a snow of perfumes in the air.
It is cold, very cold ...
And the irony of the little seamstresses' legs
looking like ballerinas ...
The wind is like a razor
in the hands of a Spaniard. Harlequinate! ...
Two hours ago the Sun burned through.
Two hours from now the Sun will burn through.

A St. Boob goes by, singing beneath the plantain trees,
A tra la la... The city police! Jail!
Are jails necessary
to preserve civilization?
My heart feels very sad...
While the gray of the goose-fleshed streets
chats a lament with the wind ...

My heart feels very glad!
This cocky little chill
makes me feel like smiling!

E sigo. E vou sentindo,
á inquieta alacridade da invernia,
como um gôsto de lágrimas na boca...

And I walk on. And go on feeling,
with the agitated alacrity of the winter chill,
something like the taste of tears in my mouth...

Ode ao Burguês

Eu insulto o burguês! O burguês-níquel,
o burguês-burguês!
A digestão bem feita de São Paulo!
O homem-curva! o homem-nádegas!
O homem que sendo francês, brasileiro, italiano,
é sempre um cauteloso pouco-a-pouco!

Eu insulto as aristocracias cautelosas!
Os barões lampeões! os condes Joões! os duques zurros!
que vivem dentro de muros sem pulos;
e gemem sangues de alguns milreis fracos
para dizerem que as filhas da senhora falam o francês
e tocam o *Printemps* com as unhas!

Eu insulto o burguês-funesto!
O indigesto feijão com toucinho, dono das tradições!
Fóra os que algarismam os amanhãs!
Olha a vida dos nossos setembros!
Fará Sol? Choverá? Arlequinal!
Mas á chuva dos rosais
o êxtase fará sempre Sol!

Ode to the Bourgeois Gentleman

I insult the bourgeois! The money-grabbing bourgeois,
the bourgeois-bourgeois!
The well-made digestion of São Paulo!
The man-belly! The man-buttocks!
The man who being French, Brazilian, Italian,
is always a cautious little take-your-time!

I insult the cautious aristocracies!
The kerosene lamp barons! the count Johns! the jackass-
    braying dukes!
who live inside walls never scaled;
and lament the blood of a few puny pennies
to say that their lady's daughters speak French
and play the "Printemps" with their fingernails!

I insult the fatal-bourgeois!
The undigested beans and bacon, guardian of traditions!
Down with those who count out their tomorrows!
Behold the life of our Septembers!
Will the sun shine? Will it rain? Harlequinate!
But in the rain of the rose gardens
ecstasy will always make the Sun shine!

Morte à gordura!
Morte às adiposidades cerebrais!
Morte ao burguês-mensal!
ao burguês-cinema! ao burguês-tílburi!
Padaria Suíça! Morte viva ao Adriano!
"— Ai, filha, que te darei pelos teus anos?
— Um colar... — Conto e quinhentos!!!
Mas nós morremos de fome!"

Come! Come-te a ti mesmo, oh! gelatina pasma!
Oh! *purée* de batatas morais!
Oh! cabelos nas ventas! oh! carecas!
Ódio aos temperamentos regulares!
Ódio aos relógios musculares! Morte e infâmia!
Ódio à soma! Ódio aos secos e molhados!
Ódio aos sem desfalecimentos nem arrependimentos,
sempiternamente as mesmices convencionais!
De mãos nas costas! Marco eu o compasso! Eia!
Dois a dois! Primeira posição! Marcha!
Todos para a Central do meu rancor inebriante!

Ódio e insulto! Ódio e raiva! Ódio e mais ódio!
Morte ao burguês de giôlhos,
Cheirando religião e que não crê em Deus!
Ódio vermelho! Ódio fecundo! Ódio cíclico!
Ódio fundamento, sem perdão!

Death to flabbiness!
Death to cerebral adiposities!
Death to the monthly-bourgeois!
to the movie-bourgeois! to the tillbury-bourgeois!
Swiss Bakery! Living death to the Café Adriano!
"Oh, sweetheart, what shall I give you for your birthday?"
"A necklace..." "Fifteen hundred bucks!!!
But we're starving to death!"

Eat! Oh, eat yourself up! stupefied gelatin!
Oh, moral mashed potatoes!
Oh, hairs in the nostrils! Oh, bald pates!
Hatred to regulated temperaments!
Hatred to muscular clocks! Death and infamy!
Hatred to calculation! Hatred to grocery stores!
Hatred to those without weakness or repentance,
ever and eternally the conventional samenesses!
Hands at their backs! I'll beat the rhythm! Hey!
Columns of two! First position! March!
All to the Main Jail of my inebriating rancor!

Hatred and execration! Hatred and rage! Hatred
    and more hatred!
Death to the bourgeois on his knees,
Smelling of religion and not believing in God!
Scarlet hatred! Fecund hatred! Cyclical hatred!
Fundamental hatred, without pardon!

Fora! Fú! Fora o bom burguês!...

Down and away! Boo! Away with the good bourgeois gentleman!...

Tristura

Une rose dans les ténèbres
MALLARMÉ

Profundo. Imundo meu coração...
Olha o edifício: Matadouros da Continental.
Os vícios viciaram-me na bajulação sem sacrifícios...
Minha alma corcunda como a avenida São João...

E dizem que os polichinelos são alegres!
Eu nunca em guisos nos meus interiores arlequinais!...

Paulicéia, minha noiva... Há matrimônios assim...
Ninguem os assistirá nos jamais!

As permanências de ser um na febre!

Nunca nos encontrámos...
Mas há *rendez-vous* na meia-noite do Armenonville...

Sadness

Une rose dans les ténèbres

MALLARMÉ

Deep down. Filthy my heart...
Look at the building: Continental Slaughterhouses.
Vices have corrupted me in false adulation without
 sacrifices...
My soul hunchbacked like the Avenue St. John...

And they say that clowns are happy!
I never rattle the little bells in my harlequinate interior!...

São Paulo, oh my beloved... There are weddings
 like that...
No one ever ever will attend them!

The permanences of being one in fever!

We never met...
But there are rendezvous in the midnight of the
 Armenonville...

E tivemos uma filha, uma só...
Batismos do snr. cura Bruma;
água-benta das garoas monótonas...
Registei-a no cartório da Consolação...
Chamei-a Solitude das Plebes...

Pobres cabelos cortados da nossa monja!

And we had a daughter, only one ...
Good Father Mist officiated at the baptism;
holy water of the monotonous hazes ...
I entered her name at the Registry of Consolation ...
I named her Loneliness of the Crowd ...

Poor shorn locks of our nun!

Domingo

Missas de chegar tarde, em rendas,
e dos olhares acrobáticos...
Tantos telégrafos sem fio!
Santa Cecília regorgita de corpos lavados
e de sacrilégios picturais...
Mas Jesus Cristo nos desertos,
mas o sacerdote no "Confiteor"... Contrastar!
—Futilidade, civilização...

Hoje quem joga?... O Paulistano.
Para o Jardim América das rosas e dos ponta-pés!
Friedenreich fez goal! Corner! Que juiz!
Gostar de Bianco? Adoro. Qual Bartô...
E o meu xará maravilhoso!...
—Futilidade, civilização...

Mornamente em gasolinas... Trinta e cinco contos!
Tens dez milréis? vamos ao corso...
E filar cigarros a quinzena inteira...
Ir ao corso é lei. Viste Marília?
E Filis? Que vestido: pele só!
Automóveis fechados... Figuras imóveis...

Sunday

Late arrivals at Mass, in lace,
exchanging acrobatic glances ...
So much wireless telegraphy!
St. Cecilia exudes from washed bodies
and pictorial sacrileges ...
But Jesus Christ in the wilderness,
but the priest at the Confiteor ... Contrast!
"Futility, civilization ..."

Who's playing today? ... The Paulistano Team.
Off to America Garden of the roses and kick-offs!
Friedenreich made a goal! Corner! What a referee!
Do I like Bianco? Crazy about him. Better than Barto ...
And my wonderful fellow-Mário! ...
"Futility, civilization ..."

Warmly in gasolines ... Thirty-five thousand!
Do you have ten bucks? let's go make the main drag ...
And mooch cigarettes for two weeks on end ...
You've got to go down to the main drag. Did you see
    Marilia?
And Phyllis! What a dress: practically naked!
Closed automobiles ... Motionless figures ...

O bocejo do luxo... Enterro.
E também as famílias dominicais por atacado,
entre os convenientes perenemente...
—Futilidade, civilização.

Central. Drama de adultério.
A Bertini arranca os cabellos e morre.
Fugas... Tiros... Tom Mix!
Amanhã fita alemã... de beiços...
As meninas mordem os beiços pensando em fita alemã...
As romas de Petrónio...
E o leito virginal... Tudo azul e branco!
Descansar... Os anjos... Imaculado!
As meninas sonham masculinidades...
—Futilidade, civilização.

The yawn of luxury ... Burial.
And also the wholesale Sunday families,
among the perenially proper ...
"Futility, civilization ..."

Main Jail. A drama of adultery.
Bertini tears her hair and dies.
Getaways ... Hold-ups ... Tom Mix!
Tomorrow a German film ... For free!
The young girls are disturbed from thinking about
    German films ...
The romes of Petronius ...
And the virgin's bed ... All blue and white!
Rest ... The angels ... Immaculate!
The young girls dream masculinities ...
"Futility, civilization ..."

O Domador

Alturas da Avenida. Bonde 3.
Asfaltos. Vastos, altos repuxos de poeira
sob o arlequinal do céu ouro-rosa-verde...
As sujidades implexas do urbanismo.
Filets de manuelino. Calvícies de Pensilvânia.

Gritos de goticismo.
Na frente o *tram* da irrigação,
onde um Sol bruxo se dispersa
num triunfo persa de esmeraldas, topázios e rubis...
Lânguidos boticellis a ler Henry Bordeaux
nas clausuras sem dragões dos torreões...

Mário, paga os duzentos réis.
São cinco no banco: um branco,
um noite, um ouro,
um cinzento de tísica e Mário...
Solicitudes! Solicitudes!

Mas... olhai, oh meus olhos saudosos dos ontens
êsse espetáculo encantado da Avenida!
Revivei, oh gaúchos Paulistas ancestremente!
e oh cavalos de cólera sangüínea!

The Animal Tamer

Around the Avenue. Trolley 3.
Asphalts. Vast, high fountains of dust
beneath the harlequinate of the sky gold-pink-green...
The intricate ordures of urbanism.
Manueline fillets. Baldnesses of Pennsylvania.

Outcries of Gothicism.
Ahead the sprinklers,
where a sorcerer sun is shattered
in a Persian triumph of emeralds, topazes and rubies...
Languid botticellis reading Henry Bordeaux
in the dragonless cloisters of the towers ...

Mário, pay a penny.
There are five on the bench: one white,
one night, one gold,
one consumptive gray and Mário ...
Solicitudes! Solicitudes!

But ... behold, oh my eyes longing after yesterdays,
that enchanted spectacle of the Avenue!
Revive, oh ancestrally *paulista* gauchos!
and oh horses of blood-red rage!

Laranja da China, laranja da China, laranja da China!
Abacate, cambucá e tangerina!
Guardate! Aos aplausos do esfusiante clown,
heróico sucessor da raça heril dos bandeirantes,
passa galhardo um filho de imigrante,
loiramente domando um automóvel!

Oranges, oranges, oranges!
Avocados, cambucás and tangerines!
Guardate! At the applause of the whizzing clown,
heroic heir of that lordly race of pioneers,
an immigrant's son elegantly passes by,
blondly taming a motor car!

Anhangabaú

Parques do Anhangabaú nos fogaréus da aurora...
Oh larguezas dos meus itinerários...
Estátuas de bronze nu correndo eternamente,
num parado desdém pelas velocidades...
O carvalho votivo escondido nos orgulhos
do bicho de mármore parido no *Salon*...
Prurido de estesias perfumando em rosais
o esqueleto trêmulo do morcego...
Nada de poesia, nada de alegrias!...

E o contraste boçal do lavrador
que sem amor afia a foice...

Estes meus parques do Anhangabaú ou de Paris,
onde as tuas águas, onde as mágoas dos teus sapos?
"Meu pai foi rei!
—Foi. —Não foi. —Foi. —Não foi."
Onde as tuas bananeiras?
Onde o teu rio frio encanecido pelos nevoeiros,
contando histórias aos sacis?...

Anhangabaú

Parks of the Anhangabaú in the conflagrations of
   the dawn...
Oh expanses of my wanderings!...
Nude bronze statues eternally coursing,
in a fixed disdain for velocities...
The votive oak concealed in the hauteurs
of the marble beast birthed in the *Salon*...
Itch of aesthesias in rose gardens perfuming
the tremulous skeleton of the bat...
No poetry whatsoever, no joys whatsoever!...

And the coarse contrast of the farmer
lovelessly honing his scythe...

These my parks of the Anhangabaú or of Paris,
 where are your waters, where the sorrows of your toads?
"My father was a king!"
"He was." "He was not." "He was." "He was not."
 Where are your banana trees?
 Where is your river grizzled by the mists
 telling tales to the forest imps?...

Meu querido palimpsesto sem valor!
Crónica em mau latim
cobrindo uma écloga que não sej a de Virgilio!...

My beloved and worthless palimpsest!
Chronicle in faulty Latin
overlying an eclogue which may not be from Virgil!...

A Caçada

A bruma neva... Clamor de vitórias e dolos...
Monte São Bernardo sem cães para os alvíssimos!
Cataclismos de heroísmos... O vento gela...
Os cinismos plantando o estandarte;
enviando para todo o universo
novas cartas-de-Vaz-Caminha!...
Os Abéis quási todos muito ruins
a escalar, em lama, a glória...
Cospe os fardos!

Mas sobre a turba adejam os cartazes de *Papel e Tinta*
como grandes mariposas de sonho queimando-se na luz...

E o maxixe do crime puladinho
na eternização dos tres dias... Tripudiares gaios!...
Roubar... Vencer... Viver os respeitosamentes no
    crepúsculo...

A velhice e a riqueza têm as mesmas cans.
A engrenagem trepida... A bruma neva...
Uma síncope: a sereia da polícia
que vai prender um bêbedo no Piques...

The Hunt

The mist snows ... Din of victories and frauds ...
Mount Saint Bernard without dogs for the most white!
Cataclysms of heroisms ... The wind freezes ...
Cynicisms planting the battle standard;
dispatching to the whole universe
new letters-from-Vaz-Caminha! ...
The Abels nearly all of them wretches
muddily escalading up to glory ...
Spit out your burdens!

But above the host flutter the placards of *Paper and Ink*
like great oneiric moths burning up in the light...

And the round-dance of samba crime
in the eternalization of the three days ... Convivial binges! ...
Rob ... Conquer ... Live the respectfully's in the dusk ...

Old age and wealth are alike hoarheaded.
The gears palsy ... The mist snows ...
A syncope: the police siren
which is going to arrest a drunk in the Piques district ...

Não há mais lugares no boa-vista triangular.
Formigueiro onde todos se mordem e devoram...
O vento gela... Fermentação de ódios egoísmos
para a caninha-do-O' dos progredires...

Viva virgem vaga desamparada...
Malfadada! Em breve não será mais virgem
nem desamparada!
Terá o amparo de todos os desamparos!

Tossem: O Diário! A Platea...
Lívidos doze-anos por um tostão
Tambem quero ler o aniversário dos reis...
Honra ao mérito! Os virtuosos hão-de sempre ser louvados
e retratificados...
Mais um crime na Moóca!
Os jornais estampam as aparências
dos grandes que fazem anos, dos criminosos que fazem
    danos...

Os quarenta-graus das riquezas! O vento gela...
Abandonos! Ideais pálidos!
Perdidos os poetas, os moços, os loucos!
Nada de asas! nada de poesia! nada de alegria!
A bruma neva... Arlequinal!
Mas viva o Ideal! God save the poetry!

There are no more places in the triangular belvedere.
Anthill where all bite and devour one another...
The wind freezes... Fermentation of hatreds and egotisms
for the cheap rum of progresses...

Living virgin wanders abandoned...
Ill-starred! Soon she will be neither virgin
nor abandoned!
She will have the protection of every abandonment!

They cough: The Daily News! The Parterre...
Livid twelve-year-olds for a penny
I also want to read about the birthdays of kings...
Honor to merit! The virtuous shall always be praised
and photographed...
One more crime in the Moóca district!
The newspapers print pictures
of bigwigs on their birthdays, of hoods on their
    crime days...

The 100-degrees of wealth. The wind freezes...
Desertions! Pallid ideals!
Lost are poets, youths, lunatics!
No wings whatsoever! no poetry whatsoever!
    no joy whatsoever!
The mist snows... Harlequinate!
But long live the Ideal! God save poetry!

—Abade Liszt da minha filha monja,
na Cadillac mansa e glauca da ilusão,
passa o Oswald de Andrade
mariscando génios en tre a multidão!...

Nota: —A última imagem está numa crónica rutilante de Helios . Não houve plágio. Helios repetiu legitimamente a frase já ouvida, e então lugar comum entre nós, para caracterizar deliciosa mania do Oswald.

—Abbot Liszt of my daughter the nun,
in the gentle blue-green Cadillac of illusion,
Oswald de Andrade passes by
hunting geniuses in the midst of the throng!...

Note: The last image is found in a newspaper column by Helios.
There was no plagiarism. Helios legitimately repeated the phrase
just heard, and then it became a commonplace among us to
characterize Oswald's delicious mania.

Nocturno

Luzes do Cambuci pelas noites de crime...
Calor!... E as nuvens baixas muito grossas,
feitas de corpos de mariposas,
rumorejando na epiderme das árvores...

Gingam os bondes como um fôgo de artifício,
sapateando nos trilhos,
cuspindo um orifício na treva cor de cal...

Num perfume de heliotrópios e de pôças
gira uma flor-do-mal... Veio do Turquestã;
e traz olheiras que escurecem almas...
Fundiu esterlinas entre as unhas roxas
nos oscilantes de Ribeirão Preto...

      —Batat'assat'ô furnn!...

Luzes do Cambuci pelas noites de crime!...
Calor... E as nuvens baixas muito grossas,
feitas de corpos de mariposas,
rumorejando na epiderme das árvores...

Nocturne

Lights from the Cambucí district on nights of crime ...
Hot weather! ... And the lowering thick clouds,
made from the bodies of moths,
rustling on the epidermis of the trees ...

The trolleys swish like a skyrocket,
clicking their heels on the track,
spitting out an orifice into the whitewashed gloom ...

In a perfume of heliotropes and puddles
whirls a flower-of-evil ... She came from Turkestan;
and she has circles under her eyes that obscure souls ...
She has smelted English pounds between her purple
    fingernails
in the bordellos of Ribeirão Preto ...

                        —Get-a you roast-a yams! ...

Lights from Cambucí on nights of crime ...
Hot weather! ... And the lowering thick clouds,
made from the bodies of moths,
rustling on the epidermis of the trees ...

Um mulato cor de ouro,
com uma cabeleira feita de alianças polidas...
Violão! "Quando eu morrer..." Um cheiro pesado
 de baunilhas

oscila, tomba e rola no chão...
Ondula no ar a nostalgia das Baías...

E os bondes passam como um fogo de artifício,
sapateando nos trilhos,
ferindo tim orifício na treva cor de cal...

— Batat'assat'ô furnn!...

Calor!... Os diabos andam no ar
Corpos de nuas carregando...
As lassitudes dos sempres imprevistos!
e as almas acordando às mãos dos enlaçados!
Idílios sob os plátanos!...
E o ciúme universal às fanfarras gloriosas
de saias cor de rosa e gravatas cor de rosa!...

Balcões na cautela latejante, onde florem Iracemas
para os encontros dos guerreiros brancos... Brancos?
E que os cães latam nos jardins!
Ninguém, ninguém, ninguém se importa!

A golden mulatto
with hair like lustrous wedding rings...
Guitar! "When I die..." A heady scent of vanilla

pivots, falls, and rolls on the ground...
In the air undulates the nostalgia of the Bahias.

And the trolleys pass by like a skyrocket,
clicking their heels on the tracks,
wounding an orifice in the whitewashed gloom...

—Get-a you roast-a yams!...

Hot weather!... Devils in the air
bodies of naked girls carrying...
The lassitudes of the unforeseen forevers!
and souls awakening to the hands of embracing lovers!
Idyls under the plantain trees!...
And the universal jealousy with magnificent fanfares
in pink skirts and pink neckties!...

Balconies in the pulsating caution, where Iracemas
    blossom
for rendezvous with white warriors... White?
So let the dogs bark in the gardens!
No one, no one, no one cares!

Todos embarcam na Alameda dos Beijos da Aventura!
Mas eu... Estas minhas grades em girándolas de jasmins,
Enquanto as travessas do Cambuci nos livres
Da liberdade dos lábios entreabertos!...
Arlequinal! Arlequinal!
As nuvens baixas muito grossas,
feitas de corpos de mariposas,
rumorejando na epiderme das árvores...
Mas sobre estas minhas grades em girándolas de jasmins,
O estelário delira em carnagens de luz,
E meu céu é todo um rojão de lágrimas!...

E os bondes riscam como um fogo de artifício,
Sapateando nos trilhos,
Jorrando um orifício na treva cor de cal...

       —Batat'assat'ô furnn!...

They all embark on the Promenade of the Kisses
    of Adventure!
But I ... Behind these garden fences of mine with
    pinwheels of jazmine,
Remain while the alley ways of Cambucí in the free
Of the freedom of parted lips! ...
Harlequinate! Harlequinate!
The lowering thick clouds,
made from the bodies of moths,
rustling on the epidermis of the trees ...
But on these my garden fences with pinwheels of jazmine,
The stars grow delirious in carnages of light,
And my sky is all a skyrocket of tears! ...

And the trolleys trace like fireworks,
Clicking their heels on the tracks,
Jetting an orifice into the whitewashed gloom ...

                    —Get-a you roast-a yams! ...

Paisagem N.º 2

Escuridão dum meio-dia de invernia...
Marasmos... Estremeções... Brancos...
O céu é toda uma batalha convencional de *confetti* brancos;
e as onças pardas das montanhas no longe...
Oh! para além vivem as primaveras eternas!

As casas adormecidas
parecem teatrais gestos dum explorador do polo
que o gelo parou no frio...

Lá para as bandas do Ipiranga as oficinas tossem...
Todos os estiolados são muito brancos.
Os invernos de Paulicéia são como entêrros de virgem...
Italianinha, torna al tuo paese!

Lembras-te? As barcarolas dos céus azúis nas aguas
    verdes...
Verde — cor dos olhos dos loucos!
As cascatas das violetas para os lagos...
Primaveral — cor dos olhos dos loucos!

Landscape 2

Gloom of a wintry noon ...
Dejections ... Tremors ... Whites ...
The sky is all a conventional battle of white confetti;
and the gray wildcats of the mountains in the distance ...
Oh! beyond dwell the eternal springs!

The slumbering houses
resemble theatrical gestures of a polar explorer
that the ice froze in the cold ...

Out there in the Ipiranga district the workshops cough ...
All the weary-laden are very white.
The winters of São Paulo are like the burials of virgins ...
Little Italian girl, torna al tuo passe!

Do you recall? The barcaroles of the blue skies in the
    green waters ...
Green ... the color of lunatics' eyes!
Cascades of violets down to the lakes...
Vernal ... the color of lunatics' eyes!

Deus recortou a alma de Paulicéia
num cor de cinza sem odor...
Oh! para além vivem as primaveras eternas!...

Mas os homens passam sonambulando...
E rodando num bando nefário,
vestidas de electricidade e gasolina,
as doenças jocotoam em redor...

Grande funcção ao ar livre!
Bailado de Cocteau com os barulhadores de Russolo!
Opus 1921

São Paulo é um palco de bailados russos.
Sarabandam a tísica, a ambição, as invejas, os crimes
e também as apoteoses da ilusão...
Mas o Nijinsky sou eu!
E vem a Morte, minha Karsavina!
Quá, quá, quá! Vamos dançar o fox-trot da desesperança,
a rir, a rir dos nossos desiguais!

God cut the soul of São Paulo
in an odorless gray ...
Oh! beyond dwell the eternal springs!...

But men go by sleepwalking ...
And running around in vicious gangs,
dressed in electricity and gasoline,
sicknesses frolic about...

A great open-air spectacle!
Choreography by Cocteau with rabble-rousers by Russolo!
Opus 1921.

São Paulo is a stage for Russian ballets.
Here tuberculosis, ambition, envies, crimes, dance the
     saraband,
and also the apotheoses of illusion ...
But I am Nijinsky!
And death, my Karsavina, comes!
Ha! Ha! Ha! Let's dance the foxtrot of desperation,
laughing, laughing at our unequals!

Tu

Morrente chama esgalga,
mais morta inda no espírito!
Espírito de fidalga,
que vive dum bocejo entre dois galanteios
e de longe em longe uma chávena da treva bem forte!

Mulher mais longa
que os pasmos alucinados
das torres de São Bento!
Mulher feita de asfalto e de lamas de várzea,
toda insultos nos olhos,
toda convite nessa boca louca de rubores!

Costureirinha de São Paulo,
ítalo-franco-luso-brasílico-saxônica,
Gosto dos teus ardores crepusculares,
crepusculares e por isso mais ardentes,
bandeirantemente!

Lady Macbeth feita de névoa fina,
pura neblina da manhã!
Mulher que és minha madrasta e minha irmã!
Trituração ascencional dos meus sentidos!

You

A dying flame grows thin,
deader yet in the spirit!
Spirit of a patrician lady,
who lives on a yawn between two gallantries
and only rarely on a cup of good strong gloom!

A woman taller
than the hallucinated awe
of the towers of São Bento!
Woman made of asphalt and marsh mud,
all insults in the eyes,
all invitations on that mouth mad with blushes!

Little seamstress from São Paulo,
italo-franco-luso-brasilico-saxon,
I like your crepuscular ardors,
crepuscular and therefore more ardent,
pioneer-wise!

Lady Macbeth made of fine mist,
pure morning haze!
Woman who is my stepmother and my sister!
Ascending pulverization of my senses!

Risco de aeroplano entre Mogí e Paris!
Pura neblina da manhã!

Gosto dos teus desejos de crime turco
E das tuas ambições retorcidas como roubos!
Amo-te de pesadelos taciturnos,
Materialização da Canaã do meu Poe...!
Never more!

Emílio de Menezes insultou a memória do meu Poe...

Oh! Incendiária dos meus aléns sonoros!
Tu és o meu gato preto!
Tu te esmagaste nas paredes do meu sonho!
êste sonho medonho!...

E serás sempre, morrente chama esgalga,
meio fidalga, meio barregã,
as alucinações crucificantes
de todas as auroras de meu jardim!

Line of the airplane between Mogí and Paris!
Pure morning haze!

I like your Turkish crime desires
And your ambitions twisted as swindles!
I love you with taciturn nightmares,
Materialization of the Canaan of my Poe…!
Nevermore!

Emílio de Menezes insulted the memory of my Poe …

Oh! Incendiary of my vibrant beyonds!
You are my black cat!
You were shattered on the walls of my dream!
this frightful dream!…

And you will always be, dying flame growing thin,
half lady, half whore,
the crucifying hallucinations
of all the dawns of my garden!

Paisagem N.º 3

Chove?
Sorri uma garoa cor de cinza,
muito triste, como um tristemente longo...
A casa Kosmos não tem impermeáveis em liquidação...
Mas neste largo do Arouche
posso abrir o meu guarda-chuva paradoxal,
este lírico plátano de rendas mar...

Ali em frente... —Mário, põe a máscara!
—Tens razão, minha Loucura, tens razão.
O rei de Tule jogou a taça ao mar...

Os homens passam encharcados...
Os reflexos dos vultos curtos
mancham o *petit-pavé*...
As rolas da Normal
esvoaçam entre os dedos da garoa...
(E si pusesse um verso de Crisfal
No De Profundis?...)
De repente
um ráio de Sol arisco
risca o chuvisco ao meio.

Landscape 3

Is it raining?
A gray mist smiles,
very sad, like a sadly long ...
The Kosmos doesn't have a close-out sale on raincoats ...
But on this Arouche Square
I can open my paradoxical umbrella,
this lyrical plantain tree of sea lace ...

Up ahead ... "Mário, put on your mask!"
"You're right, my Madness, you're right.
The King of Thule has flung his goblet in the ocean."

Men pass by drenched ...
Reflections of the shortened figures
stain the *petit-pavé* ...
The little pigeons from the Normal School
flutter between the fingers of the mist ...
(And what if I put a line from the *Crisfal*
In the *De Profundis*? ...)
Suddenly
a skittish sunbeam
draws a line down the middle of the drizzle.

Colloque Sentimental

Tenho os pés chagados nos espinhos das calçadas...
Higienópolis!... As Babilónias dos meus desejos baixos...
Casas nobres de estilo... Enriqueceres em tragédias...
Mas a noite é toda um véu-de-noiva ao luar!

A preamar dos brilhos das mansões...
O jazz-band da cor... O arco-íris dos perfumes..
O clamor dos cofres abarrotados de vidas...
Ombros nus, ombros nus, lábios pesados de adultério...
E o *rouge*—cogumelo das podridões...
Exércitos de casacas eruditamente bem talhadas...

Sem crimes, sem roubos o carnaval dos títulos...
Si não fosse o talco adeus sacos de farinha!
Impiedosamente...

—Cavalheiro... —Sou conde! —Perdão.
Sabe que existe um Brás, um Bom Retiro?

—Apre! respiro... Pensei que era pedido.
Só conheço Paris!

Colloque Sentimental

My feet are lacerated on the thorns of the sidewalks ...
Hygienopolis! ... The Babylons of my base desires ...
Houses in the noble style ... Bonanzas in tragedies ...
But the night is all a bridal veil in the moonlight!

The high tide of the gleams from the mansions ...
The colored jazz band ... The rainbow of perfumes ...
The clamor of coffers stuffed with lives ...
Naked shoulders, naked shoulders, lips heavy
    with adultery ...
And rouge—mushroom of putrifications ...
Armies of dress coats eruditely well-cut ...

Crimeless, thiefless the carnival of titles ...
Using so much talcum, you look like bags of flour!
Pitilessly ...

"Sir ..." "I am a count!" "I beg your pardon.
Do you know that a Braz district exists, a Bom Retiro?"

"Dammit!" I breathe ... "I thought you were begging.
I only know Paris!"

—Venha comigo então.
Esqueça um pouco os braços da visinha...

—Percebeu, hein! Dou-lhe gorgeta e cale-se .
O sultão tem dez mil... Mas eu sou conde!

—Vê? Estas paragens trevas de silêncio...
Nada de asas, nada de alegria... A Lua...

A rua toda nua... As casas sem luzes...
E a mirra dos martírios inconscientes...

—Deixe-me por o lenço no nariz.
Tenho todos os perfumes de Paris!

—Mas olhe, em baixo das portas, a escorrer...
—Para os esgotos! Para os esgotos!

—...a escorrer
um fio de lágrimas sem nome!...

"Come with me, then.
 Forget a moment your neighbor-lady's arms ..."

"You understood, did you! I'll give you a tip so shut up.
 The sultan has ten thousand ... But I am a count!"

"You see? This part of town glooms of silence ...
 No wings whatsover, no joy whatsoever ... The Moon ..."

 The street all naked ... The lightless houses ...
 And the myrrh of unwitting martyrs ...

"Let me put my handkerchief to my nose.
 I have all the perfumes of Paris!"

"But look, under the doors, slipping ..."
"Into the sewers! Into the sewers!"

"slipping
 a thread of nameless tears! ..."

Religião

Deus! creio em Ti! Creio na tua Bíblia!

Não que a explicasse eu mesmo,
Porquê a recebi das mãos dos que viveram
    as iluminações!

Catolicismo! sem pinturas de Calixto!...
    As humildades!...
No pôço das minhas erronias
vi que reluzia a Lua dos teu perdoares!...

Rio-me dos Luteros parasitais
e dos orgulhos soezes que não sabem ser orgulhos
    da Verdade;
e os mações, que são pecados vivos,
e que nem sabem ser Pecado!

Oh! minhas culpas e meus tresvarios!
E as nobilitações dos meus arrependimentos
chovendo para a fecundação das Palestinas!
Confessar!...

Nocturno em sangue do Jardim das Oliveiras!...

Religion

God! I believe in Thee! I believe in Thy Bible!

Not that I could explain it myself,
Because I received it from the hands of those who lived illuminations!

Catholicism! without paintings by Calixto! . . . Humilities! . . .
In the pit of my transgressions
I saw shining the Moon of Thy forgivenesses! . . .

I laugh at the parasitical Luthers
and the vile prides who know not how to be prides in the Truth;
and freemasons, who are living sins,
and know not even how to be Sin!

Oh! my faults and my ravings!
And the ennoblings of my repentances
raining for the fertilization of Palestines!
Confess! . . .

Nocturne in blood from the Mount of Olives! . . .

Naves de Santa Efigênia,
os meus joelhos criaram escudos de defesa contra vós!
Cantai como me arrastei por vós!
Dizei como me debrucei sobre vós!

Mas dos longínquos veio o Redentor!
E no poço sem fundo das minhas erronias
vi que reluzia a Lua dos seus perdoares!...

"Santa Maria, mãe de Deus..."
A minha mãe-da-terra é toda os meus entusiasmos:
dar-lhe-ia os meus dinheiros e minhas mãos também!
Santa Maria dos olhos verdes, verdes,
venho depositar aos vossos pés verdes
a coroa de luz da minha loucura!

Alcançai para mim
a Hospedaria dos Jamais Iluminados!

Naves of St. Iphigenia,
my knees have raised shields of defense against thee!
Sing how I dragged myself along for thee!
Tell how I bowed before thee!

But from far distances came the Redeemer!
And in the bottomless pit of my transgressions
I saw shining the Moon of His forgivenesses! ...

Holy Mary, Mother of God ...
My earth-mother is all my enthusiasms:
I would give her my riches and my hands, too!
Holy Mary, of the green green eyes,
I come to lay at your verdant feet
the crown of light of my madness!

Procure for me
the Inn of the Never Illuminated!

Paisagem N.º 4

Os caminhões rodando, as carroças rodando,
rápidas as ruas se desenrolando,
rumor surdo e rouco, estrépitos, estalidas...
E o largo côro de ouro das sacas de café!...

Na confluência o grito inglês da São Paulo Railway...
Mas as ventaneiras da desilusão! a baixa do café!...
As quebras, as ameaças, as audácias superfinas!...
Fogem os fazendeiros para o lar!... Cincinato Braga!...
Muito ao longe o Brasil com seus braços cruzados...
Oh! as indiferenças maternais!...

Os caminhões rodando, as carroças rodando,
rápidas as ruas se desenrolando,
rumor surdo e rouco, estrépitos, estalidos...
E o largo coro de ouro das sacas de café!...

Lutar!
A victória de todos os sozinhos!...
As bandeiras e os clarins dos armazens abarrotados...
Hostilizar!... Mas as ventaneiras dos braços cruzados!...

Landscape 4

The trucks rolling, the carts rolling,
rapid the streets unrolling,
hollow, raucous sound, clatters, crackles...
And the grand golden chorus of sacks of coffee!...

At the intersection the English cry of the São Paulo
    Railway...
But the windstorms of disillusion! the drop in coffee
    prices!...
The bankruptcies, threats, superfine audacities!...
The farmers flee to their homes!... Cincinato Braga!...
Far away Brazil with her arms folded...
Oh! maternal indifferences!...

The trucks rolling, the carts rolling,
rapid the streets unrolling,
hollow, raucous sound, clatters, crackles...
And the grand golden chorus of sacks of coffee!...

Fight!
Victory of all the little by-their-lonesomes!...
The ensigns and clarions of overflowing warehouses...
To war!... But the windstorms with folded arms!...

E a coroação com os próprio dedos!
Mutismos presidenciais, para trás!
Ponhamos os (Victória!) colares de presas inimigas!
Enguirlandemô-nos de café-cereja!
Taratá! e o pean de escárnio para o mundo!

Oh! este orgulho máximo de ser paulistamente!!!

And coronation with one's own fingers!
Presidential silences, keep out!
Let us gird on (Victory!) the necklaces of enemy teeth!
Let us garland ourselves in coffee beans!
Ta Ra Ta Ra! and the paean of mockery to the world!

Oh! this supreme pride in existing São Paulo-wise!!!

AS ENFIBRATURAS DO IPIRANGA

Oratório profano

O, woe is me
To have seen what I have seen, see what I see!
SHAKESPEARE

THE MORAL FIBRATURE OF THE IPIRANGA

A Profane Oratorio

O, woe is me
To have seen what I have seen, see what I see!
SHAKESPEARE

DISTRIBUIÇÃO DAS VOZES

Os Orientalismos Convencionais (escritores e demais artifices elogiáveis) — Largo, imponente coro afinadíssimo de sopranos, contraltos, barítonos, baixos.

As Senectudes Tremulinas (milionários e burgueses) — Coro de sopranistas.

O Sandapilários Indiferentes (operariado, gente pobre) — Barítonos e baixos.

As Juvenilidades Auriverdes (nós) — Tenores, sempre tenores! Que o diga Walter von Stolzing!

Minha Loucura — Soprano ligeiro. Solista. Acompanhamento de orquestra e banda.

ACOMPANHAMENTO DE ORQUESTRA E BANDA.

Local de execução: A esplanada do Teatro Municipal.
Banda e orquestra colocadas no terraplano que tomba sobre os jardins. São perto de cinco mil instrumentistas dirigidos por maestros... vindos do estrangeiro. Quando a solista canta ha silêncio orquestral — salvo nos casos propositadamente mencionados. E, mesmo

CAST OF SINGERS

The Conventional Orientalisms (writers and other praiseworthy artisans). Large, imposing, finely-tuned chorus of sopranos, contraltos, baritones, and basses.

The Palsied Decrepitudes (millionaires and bourgeoisie). Chorus of castrati.

The Indifferent Pallbearers (workmen, poor folk). Baritones and basses.

The Green-Gilt Youths (we). Tenors, always tenors! Just ask Walter von Stolzing!

My Madness. Coloratura soprano. Soloist. Orchestra and band accompaniment.

ORCHESTRAL AND BAND ACCOMPANIMENT

Place of Performance: The esplanade of the Municipal Theatre. Band and orchestra located on the terrace which overlooks the gardens. There are around five thousand instrumentalists under the baton of maestros...from abroad. When the soloist sings there is orchestral silence—except in those cases strictly

assim, os instrumentos que então resoam, fazem-no a
contragôsto dos maestros. Nos coros dos ORIENTALIS-
MOS CONVENCIONAIS a banda junta-se à orquestra.
É um *tutti* formidando.

Quando cantam as JUVENILIDADES AURIVERDES (há natural-
mente falta de ensaios) muitos instrumentos silenciam.
Alguns desafinam. Outros partem as cordas. Só agüen-
tam o *rubato* lancinante violinos, flautas, clarins, a
bateria e mais borés e maracás.

Os ORIENTALISMOS CONVENCIONAIS estão nas janelas e
terraços do Teatro Municipal. As SENECTUDES TREMU-
LINAS disseminaram-se pelas sacadas do Automóvel
Clube, da Prefeitura, da Rôtisserie, da Tipografia
Weisflog, do Hotel Carlton e mesmo da Livraria Alves,
ao longe . Os SANDAPILÁRIOS INDIFERENTES berram
do Viaduto do Chá. Mas as JUVENILIDADES AURIVERDES
estão em baixo, nos parques do Anhangabaú, com
os pés enterrados no solo, MINHA LOUCURA no
meio delas.

designated. Even so, the instruments which play at
that time do so at the displeasure of the maestros.
During the choruses of the Conventional Oriental-
isms the band joins the orchestra. It is a magnificent
tutti.

When the Green-Gilt Youths sing (there have been,
naturally, not enough rehearsals) many instruments
keep silent. Some are off-pitch. On others the strings
snap. Only the violins, flutes, trumpets, percussion
and other Indian trumpets and maracas can maintain
the soul-rending *rubato*.

The Conventional Orientalisms are stationed at the win-
dows and on the terraces of the Municipal Theatre.
The Palsied Decrepitudes are variously located on
the balconies of the Automobile Club, the City Hall,
the Rotisserie, the Weisflog Printing Company, the
Hotel Carlton and even the Alves Book Store in the
distance. The Indifferent Pallbearers scream from
the Viaduto do Chá. But the Green-Gilt Youths are
below in the parks of the Anhangabaú, with their feet
buried in the soil, My Madness in the midst of them.

Na Aurora do Novo Dia

Prelúdio

As caixas anunciam a arraiada. Todos os 550.000 cantores concertam apressadamente as gargantas e tomam fôlego com exagero, enquanto os borés, as trompas, o órgão, cada timbre por sua vez, entre largos silêncios reflexivos, enunciam, sem desenvolvimento, nem harmonização o tema: "Utilius est saepe et securius quod homo non habeat multas consolationes in hac vita."

E começa o oratório profano, que teve por nome:

As Enfibraturas Do Ipiranga.

AS JUVENILIDADES AURIVERDES

[pianíssimo]

Nós somos as Juvenilidades Auriverdes!
As franjadas flâmulas das bananeiras,
as esmeraldas das araras,
os rubis dos colibris,
os lirismos dos sabiás e das j andaias,
os abacaxis, as mangas, os cajus
almejam localizar-se triunfantemente,
na fremente celebração do Universal!...

On the Dawn of the New Day

Prelude

The snare drums announce the dawn. All of the 550,000 singers quickly clear their throats and take exaggeratedly deep breaths; while the Indian trumpets, the horns, the organ, all the percussion instruments in turn, amid long, reflective silences, play the theme without development or harmony: "Utilius est saepe et securius quod homo non habeat multas consolationes in hac vita."

And so the profane oratorio begins, that bore the name:

The Moral Fibrature of the Ipiranga.

THE GREEN-GILT YOUTHS

[pianissimo]

We are the Green-Gilt Youths!
The fringed banners of the banana trees,
the emeralds of the macaws,
the rubies of the hummingbirds,
the lyricisms of the *sabiás* and the parakeets,
pineapples, mangoes, cashews
long to station themselves triumphantly,
in the thundering glorification of the Universal! ...

Nós somos as Juvenilidades Auriverdes!
As forças vivas do torrão natal,
as ignorâncias iluminadas,
os novos sóis luscofuscolares
entre os sublimes das dedicações!...
Todos para a fraterna música do Universal!
Nós somos as Juvenilidades Auriverdes!

O Sandapilários Indiferentes

[num estampido preto]

Vá de rumor! Vá de rumor!
Esta gente não nos deixa mais dormir!
Antes «E lucevan le stelle» de Puccini!
Oh! pé de anjo, pé de anjo!
Fora! Fora o que é de despertar!

*[a orquestra num crescendo cromático
de contrabaixos anuncia...]*

Os Orientalismos Convencionais

Somos os Orientalismos Convencionais!
Os alicerces não devem cair mais!
Nada de subidas ou de verticais!
Amamos as chatezas horizontais!
Abatemos perobas de ramos desiguais!
Odiamos as matinadas arlequinais!

We are the Green-Gilt Youths!
The vital forces of our native soil,
the illuminated ignorances,
the new crepuscular suns
among the sublimes of dedications! ...
All for the fraternal music of the Universal!
We are the Green-Gilt Youths!

THE INDIFFERENT PALLBEARERS

[in a black salvo]

Enough racket! Enough racket!
These people won't let us sleep anymore!
Rather sing "E lucevan le stelle" by Puccini!
Oh! clumsy clod, clumsy clod!
Away! Away anything that might awaken us!

*[the orchestra in a chromatic crescendo
of double basses announces ...]*

THE CONVENTIONAL ORIENTALISMS

We are the Conventional Orientalisms!
The foundations must never fall again!
No ascents and no verticals whatsoever!
We love the boring flatness!
We hack down peroba trees with uneven branches!
We hate the harlequinate all-night sprees!

Viva a Limpeza Pública e os hábitos morais!
Somos os Orientalismos Convencionais!

Deve haver Von Iherings para todos os tatus!
Deve haver Vitais Brasis para os urutus!
Mesmo peso de feijão em todos os tutus!
Só é nobre o passo dos jaburus!
Há estilos consagrados para Pacaembus!
Que os nossos antepassados foram homens de truz!
Não lhe bastam velas? Para que mais luz!

Temos nossos coros só no tom de dó!
Para os desafinados, doutrina de cipó!
Usamos capas de seda, é só escovar o pó!
Diariamente à mesa temos mocotó!
Per omnia saecula saeculorum moinhos terão mó!
Annualmente de sobrecasaca, não de paletó,
vamos visitar o esqueleto de nossa grande Avó!
Gloria aos iguais! Um é todos! Todos são um só!
Somos os Orientalismos Convencionais!

As Juvenilidades Auriverdes

[perturbadas com o fabordão,
recomeçam mais alto, incertas]

Magia das alvoradas entre magnólias e rosas...
Apelos do estelário visível aos alguens...

Long live Garbage Collection and moral habits!
We are the Conventional Orientalisms!

There ought to be Von Iherings for all the armadillos!
There ought to be Vital Brasils for the vipers!
The same measure of beans in all the bean pots!
The only noble gait is that of the jabiru stork!
There are styles illustrious for Pacaembu districts!
For our forefathers were real men!
Were not candles good enough for you? Why more light!

Our choruses are all on the note of "do"!
For those off-pitch a lesson with the whip!
We wear silken capes, you just have to brush off the dust!
Daily at table we have calf's foot jelly!
Per omnia saecula saeculorum mills will have millstones!
Annually in frockcoat, never in sport coat,
we pay a visit to the skeleton of our grand Grandmother!
Glory to equals! One is all! All are one!
We are the Conventional Orientalisms.

The Green-Gilt Youths

*[perturbed by the cacophony, they
irresolutely recommence more loudly]*

Sorcery of the dawns amid magnolias and roses ...
Invocations of the starfall visible to the somebodies ...

—Pão de icaros sobre a toalha extática do azul!
Os tuins esperanças das nossas ilusões!
Suaviloquências entre as deliquescéncias
Dos sáfaros, aos raios do maior solar!...
Sobracemos as muralhas! Investe com os cardos!
Rasga-te nos acúleos! Tomba sobre o chão!
Hão-de vir valquírias para os olhos-fechados!
Anda! Não pares nunca! Aliena o duvidar
E as vascílações perpetuamente!

As Senectudes Tremulinas

[tempo de minuete]

Quem são estes homens?
Maiores menores
Como é bom ser rico!
Maiores menores

Das nossas poltronas
Maiores menores
Olhamos as estátuas
Maiores menores
Do signor Ximenes
—O grande escultor!

—Bread of Icaruses on the ecstatic table cloth of the blue!
The lovebird hopes of our illusions!
Suaveloquencies among the delinquencies
Of the wastelands, beneath the rays of the greatest sun!...
Let us defend the walls! Attack with the thistles!
Lacerate yourself on the thorns! Fall upon the ground!
Valkyries will come for the closed-eyes!
March! Never halt! Despise doubt
And vacillation perpetually!

THE PALSIED DECREPITUDES

[minuet tempo]

Who are these men?
Greater lesser
How good it is to be rich!
Greater lesser

From our easy chairs
Greater lesser
We look at the statues
Greater lesser
Of signor Ximenes
—The great sculptor!

Só admiramos os célebres
e os recomendados tambem!
Quem tem galeria
terá um Bouguereau!
Assinar o Lírico?
Elegância de preceito!
Mas que paulificância
Maiores menores
o Tristão e Isolda!
Maiores menores

Preferimos os coros
Dos Orientalis—
mos Convencionais!
Depois os sanchismos
(Ai! gentes, que bom!)
Da alta madrugada
No largo do Paiçandu!

Alargar as ruas...
E as Instituições?
Não pode! Não pode!
Maiores menores
Mas não ha quem diga
Maiores menores
Quem são esses homens
Que cantam do chão?

We admire only the famous
and the highly-recommended, too!
Whoever has a gallery
will own a Bouguereau!
Subscription to the Opera?
Elegance by precept!
But what a bore
Majors minors
Tristan and Iseult!
Majors minors

We prefer the choruses
Of the Conventional Ori—
entalisms!
Then the Sanchoisms
(Oh! my friends, how wonderful!)
Of the early early morning
In Paissandu Square!

Widen the streets ...
And Institutions?
Can't be done! Can't be done!
Majors minors
But won't anyone say
Majors minors
Who these men are
Who sing from the soil?

*[a orquestra súbito emudece,
depois duma grande gargalhada
de Timbales]*

Minha Loucura

[recitativo e balada]

Dramas da luz do luar no segrêdo das frestas
perquirindo as escuridões...
A traição das mordaças!
E a paixão oriental dissolvida no mel!...

Estas marés da espuma branca
e a onipotência intransponivel dos rochedos!
Intransponivelmente! Oh!...
A minha voz tem dedos muito claros
que vão roçar nos lábios do Senhor;
mas as minhas tranças muito negras
emaranharam-se nas raízes do jacarandá...

Os cérebros das cascatas marulhantes
e o benefício das manhãs serenas do Brasil!

[grandes glissandos de harpas]

Estas nuvens da tempestade branca
e os telhados que não deixam à chuva batisar!
Propositadamente! Oh!...
Os meus olhos têm beijos muito verdes

[the orchestra is suddenly silent, after a great outburst of laughter from the kettledrums]

My Madness

[recitative and ballad]

Moonlight dramas in the secrecy of the window cracks
investigating the darkness ...
The treachery of muzzles!
And oriental passion dissolved in honey! ...

These tides of white foam
and the immovable omnipotence of the sea-crags!
Immovably! Oh! ...
My voice has shining fingers
which will brush against the lips of the Lord;
but my raven-black locks
got entangled in the roots of the jacarandá tree ...

The brains of the swirling cascades
and the boon of the serene mornings of Brazil!

[great glissandi from the harps]

These clouds of the white storm
and the roofs which do not allow the rain to baptize!
Purposefully! Oh! ...
My eyes have green green kisses

que vão cair às plantas do Senhor;
mas as minhas mãos muito trémulas
apoiaram-se nas faldas do Cubatão…

Os cérebros das cascatas marulhantes
E o benefício das manhãs solenes do Brasil!
> *[notas longas de trompas]*

Estas espigas da colheita branca
e os escalrachos roubando a uberdade!
Enredadamente! Oh!…
Os meus j oelhos têm quedas muito crentes
que vão bater no peito do Senhor;
mas os meus suspiros muito louros
entreteceram-se com a rama dos cafezais…

Os cérebros das cascatas marulhantes
e o benefício das manhãs gloriosas do Brasil!
> *[harpas, trompas, orgão]*

AS SENECTUDES TREMULINAS

> *[iniciando uma gavota]*

Quem é essa mulher!
É louca, mas louca
pois anda no chão!

which will fall at the feet of the Lord;
but my very tremulous hands
were sheltered on the lap of the Cubatão...

The brains of the swirling cascades
And the boon of the solemn mornings of Brazil!

[long notes from the horns]

These ears of corn from the white harvest
and the torpedo grass robbing fertility!
Enmeshedly! Oh!...
My knees have pious falls
which will strike the breast of the Lord;
but my blond blond sighs
got interwoven with the branches of the coffee
    plantations...

The brains of the swirling cascades
and the boon of the glorious mornings of Brazil!

[harps, horns, organ]

THE PALSIED DECREPITUDES

[beginning a gavotte]

Who is that woman?
She is mad, quite mad
because she is crawling on the ground!

As Juvenilidades Auriverdes

[num crescendo fantástico]

Ódios, invejas, infelicidades!...
Crenças sem Deus! Patriotismos diplomáticos!
Cegar!
Desvalorização das lágrimas lustrais!
Nós não queremos mascaradas! E ainda menos
cordões "Flor-do-Abacate" das superfluidades!
Os tumultos da luz!... As lições dos maiores!...
E a integralização da vida no Universal!
As estradas correndo todas para o mesmo final!...
E a pátria simples, una, intangivelmente
Partindo para a celebração do Universal!
Ventem nossos desvarios fervorosos!
Fulgurem nossos pensamentos dadivosos!
Clangorem nossas palavras prof éticas
Na grande profecia virginal!
Somos as Juvenilidades Auriverdes!
A passiflora! o espanto! a loucura! o desejo!
Cravos! mais cravos para nossa cruz!

Os Orientalismos Convencionais

*[Tutti. O crescendo é resolvido
numa solene marcha fúnebre]*

Para que cravos? Para que cruzes?
Submetei-vos à metrificação!

The Green-Gilt Youths

> *[in a fantastic crescendo]*

Hatreds, envies, wretchednesses! ...
Godless beliefs! Diplomatic patriotisms!
Go blind!
Devaluation of the purifying tears!
We do not want masquerades! And even less
the "Avocado-Flower" carnival clubs of superfluities!
The tumults of light! ... The lessons of our elders! ...
And the integralization of life in the Universal!
All roads coursing to the same end! ...
And the simple homeland, one, intangibly
departing for the celebration of the Universal!
Let our zealous hallucinations bluster!
Let our generous thoughts shine!
Let our prophetic words din
in the great virginal prophecy!
We are the Green-Gilt Youths!
The passion flower! Terror! Madness! Desire!
Nails! more nails for our cross!

The Conventional Orientalisms

> *[Tutti. The crescendo is resolved
> in a solemn funeral march]*

Why nails? Why crosses?
Submit yourselves to metrification.

A verdadeira luz está nas corporações!
Aos maiores: serrote; aos menores: o salto...
E a glorificação das nossas ovações!

As Juvenilidades Auriverdes

[num clamor]

Somos as Juvenilidades Auriverdes!
A passiflora! o espanto! a loucura! o desejo!
Cravos! mais cravos para nossa cruz!

Os Orientalismos Convencionais

[a tempo]

Para que cravos? Para que cruzes?
Submetei-vos à poda!
Para que as artes vivam e revivam
Use-se o regime do' quartel!
É a riqueza! O nosso anel de matrimônio!
E as fecundidades regulares, reflectidas ....
E os perenementes da ligação mensal...

As Senectudes Tremulinas

[aos miados de flautim impotente]

Bravíssimo! Bem dito! Sai azar!
Os perenementes da ligação anual!

The true light is in the corporations!
The tall ones: saw them down; the short ones: give them
　　elevator shoes ...
And the glorification of our ovations!

The Green-Gilt Youths

[in a din]

We are the Green-Gilt Youths!
The passion flower! Terror! Madness! Desire!
Nails! more nails for our cross!

The Conventional Orientalisms

[a tempo]

Why nails? Why crosses?
Submit yourselves to the pruning knife!
So that the arts may live and relive
Employ the regimen of the barracks!
That is wealth! Our wedding ring!
And the regular fecundities, pondered ...
And the perennialies of monthly liaison ...

The Palsied Decrepitudes

[to the meows of an impotent piccolo]

Bravo! Well said! Apropos!
The perennialies of annual liaison!

As Juvenilidades Auriverdes

[berrando]

Somos as Juvenilidades Auriverdes!
A passiflora! o espanto! a loucura! o desejo!
Cravos! mais cravos para nossa cruz!

Os Orientalismos Convencionais

[da capo]

Para que cravos? Para que cruzes?
Universalizai-vos no senso comum!
Senti sentimentos de vossos pais e avós!
Para as almas sempre torresmos cerebrais!
E a sesta na rede pelos meios-dias!
Acordar às seis ; deitar ás vinte e meia;
and o banho semanal com sabão de cinza,
Limpando da terra, calmando as erupções...
E a dignificação bocejal do mundo sem estações!...
Primavera, inverno, verão, outono...
Para que estações?

As Juvenilidades Auriverdes

[já vociferantes]

Cães! Piores que cães!
Somos as Juvenilidades Auriverdes!

The Green-Gilt Youths

[roaring]

We are the Green-Gilt Youths!
The passion flower! Terror! Madness! Desire!
Nails! more nails for our cross!

The Conventional Orientalisms

[da capo]

Why nails? Why crosses?
Universalize yourselves in common sense!
Have the sentiments of your fathers and grandfathers!
For souls always cerebral cracklings!
And the noonday nap in the hammock!
Up at six; to bed at 8:30;
and the weekly bath with lye soap,
Cleaning off the dirt, salving skin eruptions …
And the yawning dignification of the world
    without seasons! …
Spring, winter, summer, autumn …
What use seasons?

The Green-Gilt Youths

[now screaming]

Dogs! Worse than dogs!
We are the Green-Gilt Youths!

Vós, burros! malditos! cães! piores que cães!

OS ORIENTALISMOS CONVENCIONAIS

[sempre marcha fúnebre, cada vez mais forte porém]

Para que burros? Para que cães?
Produtividades regulares. Vivam as maleitas!
Intermitências de polegadas certas!
Nas arquiteturas renascença gálica;
Na música Verdi; na escultura Fídias;
Corot na pintura; nos versos Leconte;
Na prosa Mace do, D'Annunzio e Bourget!
E na vida enfim, eternamente eterna,
Concertos de meia à luz do lampeão,
Valsas de Godard no piano alemão,
Marido, mulher, as filhas, o noivo...

AS JUVENILIDADES AURIVERDES

[numa grita des compassada]

Malditos! Boçais! Cães! Piores que cães!
Somos as Juvenilidades Auriverdes!
A passiflora!... Vós, malditos! boçais!

You, jackasses! Damn you! dogs! worse than dogs!

THE CONVENTIONAL ORIENTALISMS

*[still a funeral march, however
gradually louder and louder]*

Why jackasses? Why dogs?
Ordered productivities. Long live malarias!
Intermittent chills of measured inches!
In architectures, French Renaissance;
In music, Verdi; in sculpture, Phidias;
Corot in painting; in verse, Leconte;
In prose, Macedo, D'Annunzio and Bourget!
And in life finally, eternally eternal,
Lamplight concerts while the ladies knit,
Waltzes by Godard on the German piano,
Husband, wife, their daughters, the fiancé ...

THE GREEN-GILT YOUTHS

[shouting in irregular cadence]

Damn you! Dolts! Dogs! Worse than dogs!
We are the Green-Gilt Youths!
The passion flower! ... You, damn you! Dolts!

Os Orientalismos Convencionais

[*fff*]

... O corso aos domingos, o chá no Trianon ...
E as......... cidades, as......... cidades,
as......... cidades, as......... cidades,
e mil......... cidades ...¹

As Juvenilidades Auriverdes

[*ffff*]

Seus borras! Seus bêbedos! Infames! Malditos!
A plassiflora! o espanto! a loucura! o d...

Os Orientalismos Convencionais

[*fffff*]

... e as perpetuidades
Das celebridades das nossas vaidades;
Das antiguidades ás actualidades,
Ao fim das idades sem desigualdades
Quem ha-de...

---

1. Aqui o leitor, si for partidário dos Orientalismos, porá nomes de escritores paulistas que aprecia, si das Juvenilidades, os que detesta.
Exemplo com meu próprio nome: E as mariocidades. Não existe esse sufixo: quero assim para bater milhor o ritmo.

THE CONVENTIONAL ORIENTALISMS

[*fff*]

… The promenade on Sundays, tea in the Trianon …
And the ……… cities, the ……… cities,
the ……… cities, the ……… cities,
and a thousand ……… cities …[1]

THE GREEN-GILT YOUTHS

[*ffff*]

You scoriae! You drunks! Wretches! Damn you!
The passion flower! Terror! Madness! The dev…

THE CONVENTIONAL ORIENTALISMS

[*fffff*]

… and the perpetuities
Of the celebrities of our vanities;
From antiquities to propinquities,
To the end of the ages without inequalities
He who will …

---

1. Here the reader, if he is a partisan of the ORIENTALISMS, will put the names of São Paulo writers whom he admires; if a partisan of the YOUTHS, those whom he despises. An example with my own name: And the Máriocities. That suffix doesn't exist: I want it that way only to beat out the rhythm better.

As Juvenilidades Auriverdes

[loucos, sublimes, tombando exaustos]

Seus....................!!!
 (A maior palavra feia que o leitor conhecer.)
Nós somos as Juvenilidades Auriverdes!
A passiflora! o espanto!... a loucura! o desejo!...
Cravos!... Mais cravos... para... a nossa...

[Silêncio. Os Orientalismos Convencionais, bem como As Senectudes Tremulinas e Os Sandapilários Indiferentes fugiram e se esconderam, tapando os ouvidos à grande, à maxima Verdade. A orquestra evaporou-se, espavorida. Os maestri sucumbiram. Caiu a noite, aliás; e na solidão da noite das mil estrelas As Juvenilidades Auriverdes, tombadas no solo, chorando, chorando o arrependimento do tresvario final.]

Minha Loucura

[suavemente entoa a cantiga de adormentar]

Chorai! Chorai! Depois dormi!
Venham os descansos veludosos
Vestir os vossos membros!... Descansai!
Ponde os lábios na terra! Ponde os olhos na terra!
Vossos beijos finais, vossas lágrimas primeiras
Para a branca fecundação!
Espalhai vossas almas sobre o verde!

THE GREEN-GILT YOUTHS

[mad, sublime, falling exhausted]

You..................!!!
        (The filthiest word that the reader knows)
We are the Green-Gilt Youths!
The passion flower! Terror! Madness! Desire!
Nails!... More nails...for...our...

> *[Silence. The CONVENTIONAL ORIENTALISMS, as well as the PALSIED DECREPITUDES and the INDIFFERENT PALLBEARERS, have fled and hidden themselves, covering their ears against the great, the supreme Truth. The orchestra has vanished in fright. The maestri have succumbed. Night has fallen, besides; and in the solitude of the thousand-starred night the GREEN-GILT YOUTHS, having fallen to the ground, are weeping, weeping their repentance for the final delirium.]*

MY MADNESS

[softly chants the lullaby]

Weep! Weep! Then sleep!
Let velvety repose come
To vest your flesh!... Rest now!
Put your lips on the earth! Put your eyes on the earth!
Your final kisses, your first tears
For the white fecundation!
Strew your souls upon the green!

Guardai nos mantos de sombra dos manacás
Os vossos vagalumes interiores!
Inda serão um Sol nos ouros do amanhã!
Chorai! Chorai! Depois dormi!

A mansa noite com seus dedos estelare s
Fechará nossas pálpebras...
As vésperas do azul!...
As milhores vozes para vosso adormentar!
Mas o Cruzeiro do Sul e a saudade dos martírios...
Ondular do vai-vem! Embalar do vai-vem!
Para a restauração o vinho dos nocturnos!...
Mas em vinte anos se abrirão as searas!
Virão os setembros das floradas virginais!
Virão os dezembros do Sol pojando os grânulos!
Virão os fevereiros do café-cereja!
Virão os marços das maturações!

Virão os abris dos preparativos festivais!
E nos vinte anos se abrirão as searas!
E virão os maios! E virão os maios!
Rezas de Maria... Bimbalhadas... Os votivos...
As preces subidas... As graças vertidas...
Tereis a cultura da recordação!
Que o Cruzeiro do Sul e a saudade dos martírios
Plantem-se na tumba da noite em que sonhais...

Keep in the mantles of shade of the raintrees
Your interior fireflies!
There will still be a sun on tomorrow's gold!
Weep! Weep! Then sleep!

The tender night with her starry fingers
Will close our eyes...
The vespers of the blue!...
The finest voices for your cradle song!
But the Southern Cross and the recollected martyrdoms...
Undulation of the ebb and flow! Cradling of the ebb and
    flow!
For strength the wine of the nocturnes!...
But in twenty years the sown fields will blossom!
The Septembers of the virginal burgeonings will come!
The sun-drenched Decembers swelling the grain will come!
The coffee-bean Februaries will come!
The Marches of the ripening will come!

The Aprils of festive preparations will come!
And in those twenty years the sown fields will blossom!
And the Mays will come! And the Mays will come!
Prayers to Mary... Chiming of bells... The pilgrims...
Supplications uplifted... Thanksgiving poured out...
You will have the harvest of remembrance!
Let the Southern Cross and the recollected martyrdoms
Be planted at the tomb of the night in which you dream...

Importa?!... Digo-vos eu nos mansos
Oh! Juvenilidades Auriverdes, meus irmãos:
Chorai! Chorai! Depois dormi!
Venham os descansos veludosos
Vestir os vossos membros!... Descansai!

Diuturnamente cantareis e tombareis.
As rosas... As borboletas... Os orvalhos...
O todo-dia dos imolados sem razão...
Fechai vossos peitos!
Que a noite venha depor seus cabelos aléns
Nas feridas de ardor dos cutilados!
E enfim no luto em luz, (Chorai!)
Das práias sem borrascas, (Chorai!)
Das florestas sem traições de guaranis
(Depois dormi!)
Que vos sepulte a Paz Invulnerável!
Venham os descansos veludosos
Vestir os vossos membros... Descansai!

[quasi a sorrir, dormindo]

Eu... os desertos... os Caíns... a maldição...

[As JUVENILIDADES AURIVERDES e MINHA LOUCURA adormecem eternamente surdas; enquanto das janelas de palácios, teatros, tipografias, hoteis—escancaradas, mas cegas—cresce uma enorme vaia de assovios, zurros, patadas.]

Does it matter?!... I tell you gently
Oh! Green-Gilt Youths, my brothers:
Weep! Weep! Then sleep!
Let velvety repose come
To vest your flesh!... Rest now!

Long shall you sing and fall.
The roses... The butterflies... The dews...
The all-day of those sacrificed without cause...
Close up your breasts!
Let the night come to deposit her yonder hair
In the wounds of ardor of the gashed!
And finally in the brightest mourning, (Weep!)
Of the stormless beaches, (Weep!)
Of the jungles without Guarani treacheries
(Then sleep!)
Let Invulnerable Peace make your sepulchre!
Let velvety repose come
To vest your flesh... Rest now!

[almost smiling, sleeping]

I... the wilderness... The Cains... the curse...

> *[The Green-Gilt Youths and My Madness sleep eternally deaf; meanwhile, from the windows of the palaces, theatres, print shops, hotels—wide-open, but blind—there comes the enormous derision of whistles, cat-calls, and stamping of feet.]*

FIM

LAUS DEO!

THE END

LAUS DEO!

THE EMPYREAN SERIES

---

about The Empyrean Series is an imprint of Sublunary Editions, dedicated to producing new editions of overlooked works from the history of world literature.

editors Jacob Siefring, Joshua Rothes

design Joshua Rothes

web sublunaryeditions.com/empyrean

etc. Empyrean Series titles are printed on acid-free, post-consumer paper.

THE EMPYREAN CATALOGUE

1. **Three Dreams /** Jean Paul & Laurence Sterne
2. **Vagaries Malicieux /** Djuna Barnes
3. **The Last Days of Immanuel Kant /** Thomas De Quincey
4. **Maria Wutz /** Jean Paul
5. **If You Had Three Husbands /** Gertrude Stein
6. **Fantasticks /** Nicholas Breton
7. **Ivan Moscow /** Boris Pilnyak
8. **Poems /** Karl Kraus
9. **Newton's Brain /** Jakub Arbes
10. **A Looking Glasse for the Court** / Antonio de Guevara
11. **Morning Star /** Ada Negri
12. **A Cypresse Grove /** William Drummond of Hawthornden
13. **Zorrilla, the Poet /** José Zorrilla
14. **Poems /** Miguel de Unamuno
15. **Essays, Paradoxes, Soliloquies /** Miguel de Unamuno
16. **Joan of Arc /** Jules Michelet & Thomas De Quincey
17. **Pages from the Diary of a Jackass /** Ante Dukić
18. **Prefaces /** Jean Paul
19. **The City of Dreadful Night & Other Writings /** James Thomson
20. **The Collected Works /** Kathleen Tankersley Young
21. **Exercises /** Benjamín Jarnés
22. **At the Doors & Other Stories /** Boris Pilnyak
23. **Sonnets and Poems /** Antero de Quental

24. **Gebir /** Walter Savage Landor
25. **Hallucinated City /** Mário de Andrade